ONE WEEK LOAN

For Emma and Talia

News Coverage *of* Violence Against Women

Engendering Blame

Marian Meyers

SAGE Publications

International Educational and Professional Publisher

Thousand Oaks   London   New Delhi

For information address:

 SAGE Publications, Inc.
2455 Teller Road
Newbury Park, California 91320
Telephone: (805) 499-0721
Email: order@sagepub.com

SAGE Publications Ltd.
6 Bonhill Street
London EC2A 4PU
United Kingdom

SAGE Publications India Pvt. Ltd.
M-32 Market
Greater Kailash I
New Delhi 110 048 India

Printed in the United States of America

Library of Congress Cataloging-in-Publication Data

Meyers, Marian, 1954-
    News coverage of violence against women: engendering blame/
Marian Meyers.
        p. cm.
    Includes bibliographical references (p.   ) and index.
    ISBN 0-8039-5635-5 (cloth: acid-free paper).—ISBN 0-8039-5636-3
(pbk.: acid-free paper)
        1. Crime and the press. 2. Women—Crimes against. 3. Women in
    the press. I. Title.
PN4784.C8M49 1997   96-25357
070.4'4936288'082—dc20

This book is printed on acid-free paper.

97 98 99 00 10 9 8 7 6 5 4 3 2 1

Sage Production Editor: Sherrise Purdum
Sage Typesetter: Marion S. Warren

Contents

Preface

It is my hope that this book will serve as both a source of information to those concerned about violence against women and an inducement for reporters and editors to critique their coverage of this violence and to more thoughtfully write about it. The predominant problems with news about violent crime against women—such as blaming the victim and reinforcing harmful cultural stereotypes and myths—lie not with individual journalists but with the social structures and values that deny male violence against women in a serious, systemic problem rooted in misogyny and patriarchy. By reflecting this cultural blindness, the news reinforces it—and thereby contributes to the perpetuation of violence against women.

Although the problem may be systemic, individual journalists must take responsibility for changing this situation. They must, quite simply, become sensitive to the needs of the victim and to their role in fostering damaging stereotypes and myths.

There is, of course, precedent to what is being proposed here. Journalists daily are confronted with having to weigh information for possible inclusion in a story against the effects that information might have on crime victims and others. Most journalist, for example, do not routinely identify race in crime coverage, and many attempt to avoid the most egregious racial stereotyping of African Americans and the African American community. Similarly, in the coverage of male violence against women, reporters and editors must learn to avoid both the infliction of further injury on individual women as well as the perpetuation of myths and stereotypes. At the very least, this means excluding information with little journalistic value that is personally demeaning or painful to the women. It also means not representing them as in some way contributing to or being responsible for their own victimization.

Of course, to accomplish this, journalists must educate themselves about violence against women and the cultural myths that underlie this violence. News Coverage of Violence Against Women is offered as a contribution to that process.

Marian Meyers

Acknowledgments

I am indebted to many people who have helped make this book possible. I am grateful, in particular, to Carolyn Byerly and Pat Priest, both academics and activists in the movement to end violence against women, for taking the time and care to thoughtfully read and comment on the entire manuscript. This book has benefited immensely from their efforts.

I also would like to thank Mary D'Avanzo and Carolyn Lea for their research assistance, as well as the students in my "women and media" classes who, over the years, have in various ways assisted in this project. Thanks are due, too, to Susan Ford Neel, who helped with the statistical analysis of television news coverage that appears in Chapter 4, and to Linda Steiner, who provided very helpful comments on an early version of Chapter 6.

The news reporters and the advocates for raped and battered women, who so graciously agreed to be interviewed (often by students), have my sincere gratitude. Much of this book would have been impossible without them.

The photo of Louvale Westbrooks reprinted in Chapter 3 appears courtesy of the *Atlanta Journal/Constitution* and photographer Nick Arroyo, who very graciously printed copies for me. Chapter 3 is adapted from an article that originally appeared in the Spring 1944 issue of the Journal of Communication. I am indebted to Cassandra Amesley and Mary Ellen Brown for their comments on an early draft of that article, as well as to Dick Bathrick and Gus Kaufman, both of Men Stopping Violence, for their valuable insights that led to the writing of it. Permission to use the news stories analyzed in Chapter 3 was granted by the *Atlanta Journal/Constitution*. Permission to quote from the 11 p.m. newscasts also was granted courtesy of WAGA-TV and WSB-TV.

I would like to thank, too, the Department of Communication at Georgia State University for providing me with course release time and student assistance for this project.

Finally, I would like to thank my husband, Danny, for the infinite ways in which he encouraged and supported me in the writing of this book.

C H A P T E R

1

News, Violence, and Women

A Cobb County man convicted of murdering his AIDS-stricken girlfriend now faces a life sentence in prison. Ed Colantuno admitted that he shot Nicole Boswell, but claimed it was self-defense. Defense attorneys claim the victim became enraged when she found out Colantuno was leaving her. They say she attacked him with a kitchen knife and he was forced to shoot her in order to save his own life. But the jury didn't agree, finding Colantuno guilty of murder. Defense attorneys say they will appeal.

A man who took his estranged wife hostage at gunpoint is in the College Park jail tonight. Police say 34-year-old Lamar Tony argued with his wife at a bank and then forced her to go with him to a spot several blocks away. He was holding her under a tree on Main Street when police arrived. At some point in the abduction, Mrs. Tony was shot in the foot, but not seriously hurt. After a three-hour standoff, police persuaded the man to put down the gun and surrender. He is being held without bond.

We have new information tonight on yesterday's murder at the Shady Rest Hotel. We can tell you the victim's name was Faith Albert. She was 36 years old, and whoever took her life did so by beating Faith to death. She lived at the hotel. Her body was discovered by her husband.

These three news stories were aired by three major television stations in Atlanta, Georgia, during the summer of 1991. All three stories deal with violence against women in the metropolitan Atlanta area. When examined closely, they all raise troubling questions about the representation of women who are the victims of male violence.

Does it make a difference, for example, that Nicole Boswell is identified, in the very first sentence, as "AIDS-stricken," a point made much of during the trial by the defense but considered irrelevant by the prosecution? Does this identification impute guilt by raising questions about whether her behavior caused AIDS? Is it significant that the defense's position was present in four of the story's six sentences, whereas the prosecution's arguments were omitted?

What does it mean that Lamar Tony's wife appears to have no first name, that she is identified only in terms of her relationship to him—as "his wife" or "Mrs. Tony"? Is it accurate to state that she was "not seriously hurt," considering that she was shot in the foot and psychologically traumatized, in fear for her life, for at least three hours while a gun was pointed at her?

Finally, why is Faith Albert identified only by her first name when the news anchor states that "whoever took her life did so by beating Faith to death"? Does it mean anything that the use of first names in journalism is generally reserved for children, women, and pets and that had Faith Albert been a man, she would almost certainly have been identified in that statement as simply "Albert"?

These questions are more than rhetorical. How the news media represent violence against women is important not only because the news shapes our view and understanding of the world around us but also because it affects how we live our lives. This is particularly true for local news programs, which, by presenting the conditions and dangers within our own communities, "in all likelihood help to construct the audience's sense of well-being and community threat in a way that the more distant and abstracted national news cannot" (Entman, 1990, p. 335).

The news warns women about what actions and locations are unsafe, influencing decisions about where to go, what to wear, how to act, how late to stay out. It tells all of us how society views male acts of violence directed at women, delimiting what may be acceptable or unacceptable behavior for both women and men.

Of course, news coverage of violence against women cannot be divorced from news coverage of women in general. That coverage, according to feminist scholars, is the product of a male perspective that perpetuates stereotypes and myths about women while ridiculing and trivializing their needs and concerns (Mills, 1988; Molotch, 1978; Sanders & Rock, 1988; Tuchman, 1978; Tuchman, Daniels, & Benet, 1978). Recent studies (Women, Men and Media Project, 1994, 1995) also indicate that women are underrepresented within the news, in terms of both reporter bylines and their appearance as sources within the news.[1]

About the Book

This book demonstrates how the news draws on traditional notions of appropriate gender roles in the representation of violence against women. Those notions are rooted in patriarchy, which is the systemic institutionalization of women's inequality within social, political, economic, and cultural structures. The book also illustrates how qualitative, textual analysis can be used to disclose the underlying ideology, myths, and assumptions within the news.

This book presents original research in an attempt to answer the following questions: How are women who are the victims of male violence represented? How are women who successfully defend themselves against men portrayed? How do journalists negotiate the overwhelming flood of violent crimes against women to determine which ones are worth reporting and which are not? How can news coverage be improved?

These questions are examined within the context of the links between gender, race, and class as they reflect and reproduce the dominant ideology—that is, the prevailing opinions and views within society. In addition, the book expands on current theory and research about crime news. Previous research into crime reporting concluded that the news portrays criminals as deviants deserving of society's censure. However, the studies on which this conclusion was based ignored the victimization of women and therefore may be applicable only when the victim is male.

As this book will show, when women are on the receiving end of male violence, it is often *they*, not the perpetrator, who appear to be deviants worthy of condemnation. Thus, this book makes a case for the reexamination of crime news from a feminist perspective and for a broadening of traditional understandings of the social construction of news to include issues of gender, race, and class.

The focus of the research presented here is on local news in Atlanta, Georgia. Local news is more likely to report violence against women than is network news, which tends to be limited to the most sensational or celebrity-linked cases—such as the murder trial of former football star O. J. Simpson, who was acquitted of slaying his ex-wife, Nicole Brown Simpson, and her friend, Ronald Goldman, or the rape trials of boxer Mike Tyson or William Kennedy Smith of the political Kennedy clan. Local news, on the other hand, focuses more on the common, noncelebrity violence that many women experience, although even local news does not capture the most frequent forms of violence because they are so commonplace, they are not considered newsworthy. (See Chapter 6 for a discussion of how reporters determine newsworthiness.)

A number of factors virtually guarantee conformity in news content and presentation among mainstream news organizations across the United States. These factors include (a) the structure and function of media markets; (b) the common socialization of journalists; (c) the universality of news values, codes, and conventions; and (d) the role of media outlets as professional stepping-stones for journalists who have arrived from smaller markets and are on their way to larger ones. Thus, although this book examines news coverage in Atlanta, it is likely that the news stories analyzed and the views of the reporters interviewed do not differ substantially from the news or journalistic perspectives present in other big-city media markets.

Atlanta was considered a particularly good site for research into news coverage of violence against women for three reasons: (a) It is among the most violent cities in the United States; (b) its population is approximately two-thirds African American, with the larger metropolitan area about one-fourth African American[2]; and (c) it has a large population of poor people. It therefore was expected—despite reporters' reluctance to cover what they consider common occurrences (Gans, 1980; Roshco, 1975; Tuchman, 1978)—that the local news media would carry a substantial number of stories about violence against women and that these stories would provide insights into the representation of race, class, and gender.

Atlanta has consistently had one of the nation's highest homicide rates (U.S. Department of Justice, 1991, 1992, 1993, 1994a). In 1992, 198 murders were committed in the city (Federal Bureau of Investigation [FBI], 1993). In addition, Georgia ranked 10th of 50 states in the number of reported rapes ($N = 3,057$) in 1992 (U.S. Department of Justice, 1994a), with 627 in Atlanta that year (FBI, 1993). A study by the Centers for Disease Control (CDC) also found that family and intimate assaults represented 20% of the homicide reports filed in Atlanta in 1984 (Saltzman et al., 1990, p. 11). The CDC concluded that fatal and nonfatal victimization rates for African Americans and other minorities were three times the rate of those of whites. In addition, just over a quarter (27.3%) of Atlanta's 394,017 residents live in poverty, according to the 1990 federal census. Of the 102,364 below the poverty level, 88,718 (86.7%) are black and 11,239 (11%) are white.

Although Atlanta appears to be more violent than most other cities, male violence directed at women is of epidemic proportions throughout society, a part of the fabric of life in rural as well as urban and suburban communities. Statistics cannot adequately relate the cost of this violence—in terms of misery, physical and emotional pain, disfigurement, and family dysfunction, not to mention the economic costs of medical care and lost labor. The figures do, nonetheless, paint a partial picture:

■ An estimated 3 to 4 million American women are battered by their husbands and boyfriends each year (Stark et al., 1981). Although some claim that as many as half of all women will be battered at some point in their lives (Mahoney, 1991, p. 3; Walker, 1979, p. ix), others estimate that as many as two thirds of married women will be battered (Stout, 1991).

■ A total of 5,278 women were reported murdered in the United States during 1993 (FBI, 1994), up from 4,936 women the year before (FBI, 1993). Women make up 70% of all victims killed by intimates (U.S. Department of Justice, 1994c). In contrast, less than 15% of the homicides in the United States are committed by women—many of whom kill their male partners in self-defense (Browne, 1987; Walker, 1989).

■ Although 104,806 rapes were reported to law enforcement authorities during 1993 (FBI, 1994), most rapes go unreported (Koss, 1993). A truer indication of the extent of rape in the United States may be found in a victimization study (*Rape in America: A Report to the Nation*, 1992) that concluded there were 683,000 forcible rapes of women 18 years of age and older between the fall of 1989 and the fall of 1990—which means that 1.3 women are raped per minute in the United States. In addition, the U.S. Department of Justice (1994b) notes that rape by strangers, which accounts for 44% of rapes, is less common than rape by someone the woman knows, which amounts to 55% of rapes.

■ Getting out of an abusive relationship is often more dangerous than remaining in one. Separated or divorced women are 14 times more likely than married women to report having been a victim of violence by a spouse or ex-spouse, accounting for 75% of reported spousal violence (Harlow, 1991, p. 5). When battered women leave, they are at a 75% greater risk of being killed by their batterer (Hart, 1989).

Clearly, battering, rape, murder, and other forms of physical violence against women take an incalculable toll on victims, their families, and society. It is for this reason, and because news coverage of this violence shapes both public perceptions and public policy (Loseke, 1989), that this book was written.

Defining the Terrain

A number of terms used throughout this book demand explanation. In referring to violence against women, this book limits itself to physical acts of aggression directed at women by men. More specifically, it is concerned with rape, battering, murder, and other acts of physical assault that result in bodily harm to women. This is not to deny that some women are attacked by other women; however, the vast majority of acts of violence against women are the result of male behavior. In addition, this book does not address verbal sexual harassment or other forms of nonphysical threat and intimidation, which many also consider to be forms of violence. Although these acts of verbal aggression are not likely to be lethal, they nevertheless can be harmful and even devastating to women. The news, however, rarely covers nonphysical forms of violence against women, except insofar as they involve a trial or a celebrity, because the news codes and conventions for covering rape, battering, and murder differ from those involved in the reporting of nonphysical forms of violence.

When the word *women* is used in a general sense throughout this book, it refers to all females, regardless of age. The primary reason for the collapsing of ages is, quite simply, for expediency: It is quicker than frequently stating "women and girls." There is, however, another reason for this shorthand. Obviously, significant differences exist between an infant and a middle-aged woman. But there are many similarities, rooted in the subordinate relationship of females to males, that define a female's role in the world from the moment of birth. The use of the term *women* to include children as well as adults highlights those similarities.

The terms *family violence* and *domestic violence* will not be used to denote battering because these terms obscure the relationship between gender and power by failing to identify the perpetrators and victims. In fact, in 95% of the cases of domestic or family violence, the victims are women and the aggressors are men. Although Michele Bograd (1988) prefers the term *wife abuse* because it more specifically identifies the woman as the victim, this characterization also will not be used because it ignores violence in dating, which may be as prevalent as violence in marriage (Cate, Henton, Koval, Christopher, & Lloyd, 1982; Makepeace, 1981).

Suzanne Pharr (1991) has addressed the problem of terminology by suggesting the use of *sexist violence* when referring to the various forms of violence against women. "In this way," she explains, "we see that it has societal roots, and is not just any violence or hatred that occurs" (p. 2). The term *sexist violence* underscores the institutional and social nature of this violence, placing it within the context of misogyny, patriarchy, and male supremacy. It acknowledges that the violence is, in fact, sexist, that it assumes women are subordinate to men and acts on that assumption. The term *anti-women violence* also appropriately places violence against women within a social context of patriarchy and male supremacy. Both *sexist violence*[3] and *anti-women violence* will therefore be used interchangeably throughout this book.

It is also worth noting that men cannot be the victims of sexist violence, for they constitute the dominant class and their victimization can occur only within a context that differs from that defined by sexist violence. That is, men are not on the receiving end of misogynistic oppression. From a semiotic standpoint, women and men are different signs and therefore signify differently so that the brutalization of a woman by a man cannot *mean* the same thing as the brutalization of a man by another man. However, a woman caught in the cross fire of two gunmen is *not* a victim of sexist violence because the violence was not directed specifically at her by a man.

In addition, this book will most often use *victim* rather than *survivor* to describe women who have been battered, raped, or otherwise physically abused. Most counselors and advocates who work at rape crisis centers prefer the term *survivor* because they consider it more empowering and hopeful. The distinction they make is that the victims are "the recently harmed" and survivors are those who have "lived through and come to an analysis of their experience" (Byerly, 1994, p. 59).

The news, however, rarely represents women who have been brutalized as survivors, as actively resisting and defending themselves. Instead, women tend to be portrayed as passive victims who do not fight back or take other actions to protect or defend themselves. The term *victim* will therefore be used both because it more accurately describes how the news generally portrays women and because all women who have been physically assaulted are, in fact, victims.

Ideology, Myth, and Stereotype

Violence against women is framed by the news[4] so as to support, sustain, and reproduce male supremacy. Because coverage is rooted in cultural myths and stereotypes about women, men, and violence, the links between sexist violence, social structures, and gendered patterns of domination and control are disguised. The result is that the representation of women who are the victims of sexist violence polarizes around the culturally defined "virgin-whore" or "good girl-bad girl" dichotomy so that women appear to be either innocent or to blame for their victimization.

By perpetuating male supremacist ideology and the myths, stereotypes, and assumptions that underlie it, the news ultimately encourages violence against women. News reports of women as victims of sexist violence act as both a warning to women and a form of social control that outlines the boundaries of acceptable behavior and the forms of retribution they can expect for transgression. The dangers of violating the codes of behavior are gender specific, positioning all women as vulnerable to male violence and in need of protection. Indeed, the vulnerability of women is a given and, linked to questions of complicity, remains lurking in the shadows of representation. Was she where she shouldn't have been? Did she fail to take precautions—to lock a door, to arrange for security? Did she do something to provoke the attack?

Because all women who are victims of violence are represented in the news as inherently vulnerable to men, real security can be provided only by those who are not similarly vulnerable—that is, by men. Therein lies the primary, underlying contradiction in the representation of women as victims of violence: Women are made vulnerable by men, but they can be made safe only by men. Bart and O'Brien (1985) note how this contradiction, when applied to rape, reinforces the status quo by making women dependent on men: "Fear of rape makes it difficult for women to exist independently of men, because women believe they need men to protect them from other men" (p. 112).

But it is not simply fear of rape that transforms men from a potential threat to women to being their only hope for security. Women's fear of male violence is more general, more generic, and extends to all other forms of male aggression, from the battered woman who tries desperately to please her abuser for fear of another beating to the woman who appears to passively endure rape because she fears she will be further brutalized and perhaps murdered if she resists.

Individual Pathology, Social Misogyny, and Male Responsibility

The systemic nature of misogyny and patriarchy supports violence against women in both private and public ways, behind closed doors and on city streets. But it by no means excuses acts of male violence against women. To suggest that men cannot be held accountable for their acts of sexist violence because society "makes them do it" is to deny individual responsibility and free will and to obscure the role that culture plays in reinforcing this behavior. To state that men are not responsible for sexist violence because they, too, are victims of a misogynistic society is analogous to excusing the Ku Klux Klan for the burning of a cross on a black family's front lawn—a clear act of racist aggression and terrorism—on the grounds that society is racist and therefore the individual cannot be held responsible.

Likewise, the very common view that men who rape, murder, or otherwise commit acts of violence against women are "sick" or in some way pathological ignores the social roots of this violence. Jane Caputi (1993) emphasizes that our culture denies "the fundamental *normalcy*" of violence against women and attempts to "paint it as the domain of psychopaths and 'monsters' only" (p. 12). This portrayal is not confined to this side of the Atlantic: A study of sex crimes in the British press also found that the news tends to present the assailant as a monster or "sex fiend" (Soothill & Walby, 1991). The "monster" depiction, Wendy Kozol (1995) states, "ignores power relations and turns violence into something that only occurs in deranged families" (p. 657).

The representation of the assailant as a monster or psychopath also allows men to distance themselves from the perpetrators of these crimes. Scully and Marolla (1993) point out that diverting attention away from environmental variables such as culture or social structure ignores evidence that rape, as well as other forms of violence against women, is learned behavior (p. 28). Indeed, the cultural roots of sexist violence become apparent when one considers the epidemic nature of the problem. When, for example, a majority of male college students—51%—admit they would rape if they thought they could get away with it (Malamuth, Haber, & Feshback, 1980), it becomes

clear that one cannot legitimately argue for individual psychopathology as the cause of sexist violence without concurrently positing that
most men suffer from this disease.

Jane Caputi (1993), who considers the serial murder of
women "crimes of sexually political, essentially *patriarchal*, domination" (p. 13), states that "a feminist analysis would not accept
the equation that to recognize the responsibility of society for sexually political murder is to absolve the murderer" (p. 18). Rather, she
says, a feminist analysis would point to the connection between
the murderer and society, with the murderer acting as "society's henchman . . . in the maintenance of patriarchal order through
force" (p. 18).

Bart and Moran (1993), although noting that the vast majority of
mass murderers are men and their victims most often women, agree
that a man who commits mass murder is "deranged." But they point
out that "his choice of victims also reflects the misogyny being
supported in the culture" (p. 79). They refer to the problem of labeling
male violence as individual pathology in discussing what has become known as the "Montreal massacre"—the killing of 14 women
at the University of Montreal on December 6, 1989, by a man with a
rifle who evacuated the men from the classrooms before opening fire
on the women. The killer, Marc Lépine, left behind a note blaming
feminists for ruining his life. Significantly, he called the women,
students in the university's engineering school, feminists before
shooting them.

> Although the Montreal killer said that he murdered the women because
> he hated feminists, the debate that followed attributed his behavior
> simply to psychopathology, ignoring the fact that he was a woman-
> hating man reinforced by a woman-hating society. (Bart & Moran, 1993,
> p. xiii)

A number of Canadian feminists, writing about news coverage of
the massacre, similarly noted that the news media created sympathy
for Lépine by attempting to explain what happened in terms of
Lépine's unhappy personal life, by characterizing him as "sick" and
even blaming his mother (Malette & Chalouh, 1991). At the same
time, the news ignored feminist expertise on male violence, thus

camouflaging the social nature of the slaughter and diminishing its political impact.

Of course, the media's preference for psychopathological explanations for sexist violence is not limited to the Montreal massacre. It is the predominant frame offered by the news media within the United States, serving to limit discussion so that it excludes a feminist analysis that would take into account cultural and social factors such as patriarchy and misogyny.

Race and Class

Although feminist theorizing about the social role of patriarchy and male supremacy provides a framework for understanding violence against women, gender cannot be divorced from race, class, and other signifiers of domination and control in the representation of anti-women violence. Social prominence is directly related to access to the news media (Gans, 1980; Sigal, 1973) so that the more socially prominent the people involved—that is, the higher their "social ranking" (Roshco, 1975)—the more extensive and prominent the coverage. Thus, violence against women who are poor and black is less likely to receive extensive coverage (or any coverage) than is violence against women who are white, middle-class, and upper-class.

Although the race of the victim and assailant is rarely mentioned by reporters or news anchors, newspaper photographs and television visuals are often revealing, as is the location of a crime or the home address of the assailant. Atlanta's neighborhoods are largely segregated, with African Americans to the south and whites to the north. Most residents therefore can fairly accurately guess the race of a suspect or victim by the location of the crime or the home address. For example, the south side of Atlanta is code for black and generally poor, despite the fact that southwest Atlanta is home to many middle-class and wealthy African Americans. Atlanta's public housing projects, such as Carver Homes and Bankhead Courts, are considered exclusively black. On the north side of the city, the neighborhood of Buckhead and the northern counties of Gwinnett and Cobb are synonymous with rich and white, although they have, in fact, a large number of middle-class whites as well.

Discourse Analysis

In exploring the representation of anti-women violence in Chapters 3, 4, and 5, I employed a qualitative, textual analysis of stories that appeared in the *Atlanta Journal-Constitution*—which consists of the morning *Constitution*, the afternoon *Journal*, and the combined Sunday edition, the *Atlanta Journal and Constitution*—as well as stories aired on WSB, WXIA, and WAGA, which were, respectively, the ABC, NBC, and CBS television network affiliates in Atlanta at the time the study was conducted.[5]

Textual or discourse analysis[6] as a methodology pays close attention to language and its usage, exploring the discursive structures and rhetorical strategies of what is broadly termed the *text*—which could be a speech, film, television show, newspaper, photograph, book, magazine, poem, or any other social artifact imbued with meaning.[7] Discourse becomes visible or audible through the text, which can be systematically analyzed to disclose underlying meanings. The methodology "involves all the levels and methods of analysis of language, cognition, interaction, society and culture," according to Teun van Dijk (1985, p. 10), and can be used to reveal "underlying personal or social patterns as they are expressed or indicated by text and talk" (p. 11). When critically applied to the news, discourse analysis examines the discursive mechanisms— topics, overall schematic forms, local meanings, style, and rhetoric, for example—involved in the reproduction of ideology within news content (van Dijk, 1991).

Whether a story makes sense depends on what van Dijk (1991) calls "local coherence," which "depends upon our knowledge and beliefs about society" (p. 178). Thus, it is possible to examine the news for local coherence—how the discourse creates meaning that appears commonsensical—to reveal society's predominant assumptions, values, myths, and stereotypes.

Although headlines, subheadlines, and leads provide the semantic macrostructure or major topic of the text, defining, summarizing, and evaluating the most important elements of the story (van Dijk, 1988a, 1988b), it is at the microlevel of news discourse that style, meaning, and rhetoric can be examined to ascertain underlying meanings and ideologies (van Dijk, 1991, p. 176). Microlevel rhetorical devices that obscure the workings of ideology can be exposed through systematic discourse analysis. These devices include (a) vagueness, which works to conceal responsibility for negative actions; (b) overcompleteness, which adds irrelevant details; (c) presupposition; (d) concealments; (e) euphemisms; (f) blaming the victim; (g) positive self-presentation; and (h) negative other-presentation. For example, stating that "an argument began" is rhetorically vague in that it obscures who started the argument, and how, so that both parties to the argument appear to be equally at fault. As stated earlier, the term *domestic violence* is a euphemism for battering that fails to identify the gender of who is pummeling whom. Similarly, overcompleteness may be used to include details—such as that a woman was using drugs or engaged in behaviors considered socially inappropriate at the time of her abuse—that could portray the woman as somehow having contributed to her abuse.

One of the most useful and powerful analytical devices in the critical study of discourse is the "systematic analysis of implicitness" (van Dijk, 1991, p. 180). As van Dijk (1988a) explains,

> Much of the social, political or ideological relevance of news analysis resides in making explicit implied or indirect meanings or functions of news reports: What is not said may even be more important, from a critical point of view, than what is explicitly said or meant. (p. 17)

Thus, the discourse analyst must be able to, in a sense, read between the lines to expose implicit meanings that are obscured at the surface level of reading. These implied meanings, although not outwardly stated, draw on consensual understandings and stereotypes so that they need not be stated out loud to be understood.

John Fiske (1994) notes that discourse has three dimensions at the level of practice: a "topic or area of social experience to which its sense making is applied; a social position from which this sense is made and whose interests it promotes; and a repertoire of words, images and practices by which meanings are circulated and power applied" (p. 3). He points out that discourse analysis

> relocates the whole process of making and using meaning from an abstracted structural system into particular historical, social, and political conditions. Discourse, then, is language in social use; language accented with its history of domination, subordination and resistance; language marked by the social conditions of its use and its users: It is

politicized, power-bearing language employed to extend or defend the interests of its discursive community. (p. 3)

Society, Fiske adds, is multidiscursive, with various discourses battling for dominance by repressing, invalidating, and marginalizing competing discourses so that discourse itself is "a terrain of struggle" (p. 5) reflecting the interests of a hierarchy of social formations. Thus, within a capitalistic society, the discourse of capitalism remains dominant by casting alternative or oppositional discourses—social democracy or socialism, for example—as ineffective, inefficient, and unnatural. Similarly, within a society in which patriarchal ideology is deeply embedded—as is the case in the United States and, in varying degrees and permutations, in all other countries—the dominant discourse supports patriarchy and maintains its position of prominence by marginalizing feminist discourse and, therefore, feminists.

Examining the news through discourse analysis acknowledges both polysemia—that is, the inability of the text to close off a variety of meanings—and the audience member's particular "decoding" strategies, or the means by which she or he makes sense of a text (Hall, 1980). These strategies are related to the individual's understandings, background, and experiences (Morley 1980, 1985) so that any number of interpretations are possible, although a particular interpretation is privileged and most likely to shape meaning because it carries the weight of cultural assumptions and expectations.

The decoding strategies employed in this book were informed by a feminist framework that places the news within the broader social context of a patriarchal society. The analyses presented owe a debt both to feminist theory and, in particular, to the rape survivors' and battered women's movements.

The Chapters

In addition to discourse analysis, this book uses a quantitative content analysis of television news stories; in-depth interviews with newspaper, television, and radio journalists; and in-depth interviews with advocates for women who have been the victims of male violence.

Chapter 2 completes the first part of this book. It combines previous research about crime news in general and the coverage of violence against women in particular with feminist theory about anti-women violence to provide a framework for understanding the representation of violence against women in the news. It also seeks to situate this portrayal within the cultural context of race and class. In addition, the chapter examines the legal and judicial treatment of battered women who kill in self-defense as illustrative of how abused women are further victimized by social institutions.

The second section presents textual analyses of the news. Chapter 3 provides an analysis of newspaper coverage of the murder of a battered woman by her husband. It shows how myths about gender, race, and class converged to blame the woman for her own victimization by both denying that she was, indeed, a battered woman and absolving her husband of responsibility for his actions. Chapter 4 provides a quantitative and qualitative look at local television news, demonstrating the utility of both methodologies in collaboration. It shows how patriarchal ideology reflected in the good girl-bad girl or virgin-whore dichotomy determines the guilt or innocence of the *victim* rather than of her assailant.

As the section's final study, Chapter 5 explores the representation of women who have successfully defended themselves against male violence. Whether women who fight back are portrayed as justified or not in their acts of self-defense is tied to traditional understandings of appropriate female behavior.

The third section of the book concerns the process by which reporters produce the news. Chapter 6 asks how reporters and editors, as members of an interpretive community (Zelizer, 1992, 1993), negotiate and justify their decisions concerning what is newsworthy and what is not. In-depth interviews with journalists reveal their reliance on the concept of "unusualness" to determine which violent crimes against women to cover. The study suggests that the invocation of unusualness as a guiding principal allows journalists to deflect charges of gender, race, and class bias in their reporting.

Chapter 7 suggests ways in which news coverage of anti-women violence can be improved. It presents previous research about how journalists can better report news of violence against women, along with the views of 20 advocates for raped or battered women. Chapter 8 concludes the book by summarizing its findings and pointing to actions that journalists and news organizations can take to report sexist violence more accurately and fairly.

Notes

1. The most recent Women, Men and Media Project study (1995) indicates that this situation is not getting any better, with coverage of and by females leveling off.

2. According to the U.S. Bureau of the Census (1990), Atlanta's total population is 394,017, of which 264,262 residents are black and 122,327 are white. In the metropolitan statistical area, the total population is 2,833,511, of which 736,153 are black and 2,020,017 are white.

3. The terms *sexist violence* and *sexist crime* as used in this book should not be confused with *sexual violence* or *sex crimes*. The former emphasizes the social context within which the violence occurs; the latter emphasizes that the act has a sexual component, as in rape or sodomy. Others who research and write about violence against women may have different definitions. For example, some feminist analysts, such as Judith Lorber, the founding editor of the journal *Gender and Society*, broadly define sex crimes to include all "aggressive acts of sexualized violence," ranging from obscene phone calls and sidewalk catcalls to "Jack-the-Ripper serial murders and the massacre of 'feminists' by men who feel their dominance challenged" (Bart & Moran, 1993, p. xii).

4. Tuchman (1978, p. 193) explains that "news frames" transform strips of information about an event into stories by providing a context for understanding.

5. WAGA has since aligned itself with the Fox network.

6. Discourse analysis is a type of textual analysis, which is a more generic term for analyses that examine the text for underlying or hidden meaning. The terms will be used interchangeably throughout this book.

7. Buildings, clothing, cars, social rituals, and other cultural products also can be "read" as texts.

2

News and the Mythology of Anti-Woman Violence

Newsworthiness—that is, those qualities journalists believe make an event worth reporting—has never been easy to define. There are no hard-and-fast rules about what constitutes the news, and reporters and editors themselves are often vague about how they separate what to cover from what to ignore within the vast pool of occurrences that could, potentially, be news.

Organizational concerns and constraints, as well as the type of event and the routine ways journalists cover specific events, also shape reporter understandings of the news process, newsworthiness, and what makes up the news (Berkowitz, 1992; Epstein, 1974; Sigal, 1973; Tuchman, 1978). News scholars have also noted that the assessment of newsworthiness is a matter of ongoing compromise and negotiation among reporters and editors (Berkowitz, 1992; Gans, 1980; Sigal, 1973; Tuchman, 1978; Turow, 1994). For example, journalists may negotiate whether and what kind of follow-up is needed for a second-day story about a plane crash or a murder. Typically, consensus is reached within mutually recognized boundaries that guarantee that a minor accident, such as a car collision in which physical and property damage are minimal, does not become front-page news.

The negotiated circumference of newsworthiness, although somewhat permeable, is defined by what variously has been referred to as manifest values (Roshco, 1975), journalistic norms (Tuchman, 1978), the conventions of newsmaking (Sigal, 1973), and enduring values (Gans, 1980). Newsworkers share an "allegiance to professionally shared values" (Gans, 1980, p. 79) that, Liesbet van Zoonen (1994) points out, "facilitates decision making, and as such is instrumental to a media organization's efficiency" (p. 56). Indeed, the collective context of media production provides the basis of a socialization process through which the newsworker "has to cooperate with colleagues, has to take specific needs, routines and traditions of the organization into account, and is limited by the social, economic and legal embedding of the media institution" (van Zoonen, 1994, p. 49).

A Critical View of News

News scholars also note that the values, norms, and conventions that shape the news support the status quo by representing the interests of a white, middle- and upper-class, male elite. Critical theorists, in particular, emphasize that the news supports the dominant power structure by creating a consensus that appears grounded in everyday reality (Brunsdon & Morley, 1978; Gitlin, 1980; Hall, 1977, 1982; Hall, Connell, & Curti, 1977; Hartley, 1982). The news contributes to the building and maintenance of popular consensus through the use of language that reflects and perpetuates the values, beliefs, and goals of the ruling elite. Consensus is thereby disguised so that it appears to be not the product of ideology but the result of what is simply natural or part of common sense—just the way things are and the way things are done.

Stuart Hall has noted that both gender and race appear "to be given by Nature," so that they become among "the most profoundly 'naturalized' of existing ideologies" (1981, p. 32). Patriarchy, for example, benefits from the notion that men are naturally and therefore rightfully more sexually aggressive than women, for it justifies the use of that aggression against those not similarly endowed—that is, women.

Consensus is linked to the concept of hegemony, which explains how the ruling elite maintains its position of privilege by winning the consent of the governed (Gramsci, 1971, 1983). Hegemony depends on a combination of force and consent, but it is most effective when consent is obtained through the unquestioned, unconscious acceptance of ideology (Althusser, 1971). Stuart Hall (1977) explains:

> Hegemony is accomplished through the agencies of the superstructures—the family, education system, the church, the media and cultural institutions, as well as the coercive side of the state—the law, police, the army, which also, in part "work through ideology." (p. 333)

The appearance of neutrality and common sense allows those in power to maintain their position within a hierarchy of competing social formations (Gramsci, 1971, 1983). Because hegemony is never permanent, subordinate classes are never totally absorbed or incorporated into and by the dominant classes. The dominant discourse is open to being challenged and modified, and it is able to accommodate alternative meanings, values, opinions, and attitudes. Hegemony therefore must be continually renewed, fought for, re-created, and defended. Ideological struggle is thereby conceived of as a process of disarticulation and rearticulation of given ideological elements within a hierarchy of discourses. As Mouffe (1981) explains,

> The objective of ideological struggle is not to reject the system and all its elements but to rearticulate it, to break it down to its basic elements and then to sift through past conceptions to see which ones, with some changes of content, can serve to express the new situation. Once this is done, the chosen elements are finally rearticulated into another system. (p. 230)

Feminism constitutes a challenge to patriarchy's hegemony by challenging its central assumptions and rearticulating the meaning of gender. Indeed, the women's movement has continually struggled to disarticulate conventional notions of gender roles and behavior and to rearticulate them in favor of equality. This contestation of the very meaning of *woman* occurs in various forms within a variety of cultural levels and institutions—including the news.

Crime News

As with all news, crime news is guided by a common understanding of news values or imperatives. Crime news is culturally defined and reflects society's predominant values and assumptions as well as the organizational considerations and constraints of the news organization. As Gregg Barak (1994) points out, crime news reinforces particular forms of social control, with the depiction of crime, criminals, and victims changing over time to correspond with social, political, and economic changes in society: "Crime stories produced by the news media in this country reveal as much about the American experience and U.S. values as they do about crime and the administration of justice" (p. 3).

Although news reporting and coverage are culturally specific, research in Britain indicates that there are perhaps more similarities within the news in Western, industrialized, democratic societies than there are differences. For example, a study of crime news in Britain by Steve Chibnall (1977) appears to be applicable to the reporting of crime in the United States. Chibnall found that crime news is guided by eight "professional imperatives":

1. Immediacy, which robs events of their historical context
2. Dramatization, which directs attention away from the meaning of an event through emphasis on the sensational
3. Personalization, which reduces conflict over complex issues to a clash of personalities
4. Simplification, which strips an event of meaning so that it will fit into a preexisting news format
5. Titillation, which sacrifices understanding for superficial, sensational details
6. Conventionalism, which forces news events into established scenarios whether they "fit" or not

7. Structured access, which requires that stories be grounded in the authoritative pronouncements of experts within "legitimate" institutions

8. Novelty, which encourages speculation in the search for fresh news angles

Chibnall's imperatives correspond to what American sociologists (Roshco, 1975; Schudson, 1978; Tuchman, 1978) tend to refer to as news values that guide reporters in the determination of newsworthiness and the covering of news. These values include the following:

1. Timeliness
2. Conflict
3. The unexpected
4. Routine typifications
5. A preference for big "names" and official viewpoints
6. Superficial acquaintance-with information (as opposed to a more analytical knowledge-about)
7. Objectivity

News values constitute a framework that supports the dominant ideology while marginalizing, trivializing, and constructing as deviant or dangerous any challenge to it. This process is not a product of editorial conspiracy, for such complicity would destroy the basis of the media's legitimacy—that is, its " 'objectivity,' 'neutrality,' 'impartiality' and 'balance' " (Hall, 1977, p. 345). Rather, news reflects the social organization of reporting and the professional imperatives and commercial interests that are a part of it.

Besides bureaucratic and occupational factors, crime news is also informed by "the monopoly official sources have over primary information" (Sherizen, 1978, p. 205). The official experts or sources for crime news are the police, who provide an interpretation of criminality that reporters then legitimate by presenting as objective and "neutral." Because the postarrest stages of the criminal justice system—which involve the courts and prison—are seldom covered, the police act as the primary "promoters" of crime news (Molotch & Lester, 1974).

Obviously, some crimes are promoted more than others. Sanford Sherizen (1978) found that whereas almost 70% of all murders were reported in Chicago newspapers, only 5% of rapes and less than 1% of almost all other crimes became news. The rule for crime coverage, Sherizen notes, is that

> the more prevalent the crime, the less it would be reported, with the exception of murder/manslaughter. . . . The only other crimes that appeared more frequently than expected were those which were (or could be written as) humorous, ironic, and/or unusual or in which the situation was sentimental or dramatic, especially in terms of the participants. (p. 215)

In addition, critical media theorists maintain that the news portrays crime as ripping at the social fabric of community and family values (Cohen & Young, 1973; Ericson, Baranek, & Chan, 1987; Hall, Critcher, Jefferson, Clarke, & Roberts, 1978). Criminals, they claim, are presented as deviants whose actions are outside the limits of acceptable social behavior and who, therefore, deserve to be shunned by all law-abiding citizens. In this way, news stories act as morality tales that delineate appropriate social behavior and the consequences of violation. The crime-as-deviance theorists also claim that crime coverage creates a media-fed moral panic in which public fears of lawlessness and escalating crime are heightened and then used by the State to justify the imposition of a law-and-order society with tougher crime laws and a greater police presence.

Based on this scenario, one might expect the crime of violence against women to be the target of a well-orchestrated, government-sponsored, law-and-order campaign directed at eradicating this menace to family and society. After all, the fear of violence, particularly rape, circumscribes the lives of half the population, and violent crimes against women threaten the stability of families and homes.

Unfortunately, the crime-as-deviance theorists failed to examine male violence specifically directed at women. In doing so, they also failed to recognize that "the representation of violence is inseparable from the notion of gender" (DeLauretis, 1987, p. 33). Anti-woman violence—whether rape, murder, battering, or any other type of physical assault—is gendered within the context of a patriarchal society in which male domination and female subordination are considered both desirable and the norm. In sidestepping the question of gender, the crime-as-deviance theorists apparently assumed either that the representation of violence against women was no different from that of violence directed against men or that it simply was not worthy of examination.

Studies of rape, battering, and sex crime reporting indicate that crime-as-deviance theory does not apply to news coverage of violence against women. These studies show that the reporting of this violence serves as a warning and a form of social control for all women, providing them with a guide to appropriate female behavior and detailing the repercussions for violating the rules. In addition, although crime-as-deviance theory claims that the news defines and ostracizes the *criminal* as deviant, studies of news coverage of violence against women indicate that the news positions the *female victim* as deviant and deserving of condemnation if she in any way appears to have disregarded or flaunted socially approved gender roles and expectations. The result is that within the world of print and broadcast journalism, female victims tend to be depicted as either virgins or whores, good girls or bad girls.

The Mythology of Anti-Woman Violence

The good girl-bad girl dichotomy evident in news coverage of violence against women reflects patriarchal notions about the "proper" place and role of women (Benedict, 1992; Meyers, 1994; Smart & Smart, 1978; Soothill & Walby, 1991). Underlying these notions is a mythology of anti-woman violence that appears with minor variations across a variety of *types* of violence, whether rape, battering, or even murder when the perpetrator is a man.

Feminist theorists of violence against women maintain that "all forms of violence are interrelated, coalescing like a girdle to keep women . . . subordinate to men" (Bart & Moran, 1993, p. 1). Thus, rape, obscene phone calls, battering, murder, sexual harassment, torture, and other forms of both physical and nonphysical violence against women have the same end—to perpetuate male domination. Jane Caputi (1993) also argues that all acts of violence against females are hate crimes in the same way that any assault, intimidation, or act of harassment due to the victim's race, religion, or ethnic background is considered a hate crime.

Carole Sheffield (1993) uses the term *sexual terrorism* to describe "the system by which men and boys frighten, and by frightening, dominate and control women and girls" (p. 73). Acts of sexual terrorism are constituted by both real and implied violence. Thus, Sheffield states, an obscene telephone call is a form of sexual intimidation viewed as terroristic by many women, just as are sexual harassment and more direct physical assault or violence. Often, Sheffield states, the common, everyday appearance of these acts obscures their function:

> They are often readily dismissed by the women themselves and by agents of social control. . . . These common experiences, which include a range of verbal, visual and physical intrusions, are the underpinning of sexual terrorism: They serve to remind women and girls that they are at risk and vulnerable to male aggression just because they are female. (p. 73)

Sheffield (1987) has also pointed out that "all systems of oppression employ violence or the threat of violence as an institutionalized mechanism for ensuring compliance" (p. 171), with sexual terrorism "a crucial strategy in sustaining the power relationships of *patriarchy*" (p. 172). The concept of male power is interwoven throughout all interpersonal male-female interactions, constituting a "structural dimension of society" in which violence against women and other demonstrations of male power act to reproduce and maintain male dominance and female subordination (Hanmer & Maynard, 1987, p. 3). All acts of anti-woman violence can therefore be considered "acts of terrorism intended to keep all women in their place through intimidation" (Jones, 1980, p. 282).

John Stoltenberg (1989) notes that "the ethics of male sexual identity are essentially rapist" (p. 19) and are promulgated by social myths. These rape myths are inherent in the mythology of anti-woman violence: "Women want to be raped, women deserve to be raped, women provoke rape, women need to be raped, and women enjoy being raped" (Stoltenberg, 1989, p. 20). Diana Russell (1984) identifies other rape myths within the broader mythology of anti-woman violence: (a) There is no such thing as rape because if a woman didn't want to have sex she could easily avoid it; (b) rape, if it does exist, is very rare; (c) the few rapists who exist are sadistic, crazy psychopaths; (d) rape is the "natural outcome of opportunity," which is to say that if women give men the opportunity to rape them, men will naturally take it; and (e) rape is simply masculine behavior.

Mildred Pagelow (1981) notes the primary myths about battering: (a) Those involved are pathological—the woman is masochistic, the batterer is "sick"; (b) the woman provoked him; (c) the woman must have had a reason for staying; (d) battered women never press charges; and (e) battering is restricted to the "lower classes" (p. 54). She emphasizes that myths and stereotypes about battered women are pervasive and serve "to victimize the victim(s) further by stigmatizing them or helping to keep them locked in their violent relationships" (p. 88). Sheffield (1993) similarly points out that obscene phone calls embody "the patriarchal myths of rape: that women are sexually 'bad'—depraved, insatiable, lustful" (p. 78). Belief in these myths, she adds, allows men to justify their behavior with the claim that women deserve or like it.

One of the functions of the mythology of anti-woman violence is to reinforce patriarchy by obscuring or "naturalizing" the relationship of sexist violence to male supremacy. What can be called anti-woman violence because it is directed *specifically against women* by men appears to be not simply common and everyday but "just the way things are," part of the natural and correct order of the universe. Thus, battering is naturalized within the social fabric because it appears unconnected to the

> historical development of the isolated nuclear family in a capitalist society, to division of the public and private/domestic domains, to specialization of 'appropriate' male and female family roles, and to the current position of wives as legally and morally bound to husbands. (Bograd, 1988, pp. 14-15)

Even sociologists and psychologists who study or attempt to "cure" battering tend to see it not as the practice of male domination and control but as the result of family dysfunction. Traditional sociological approaches are concerned with patterns of relationships within families or between couples as well as with the culture, norms, and values guiding behavior. From this perspective, violence is seen as a response by both sexes to structural and situational stimuli.

Most psychodynamic explanations also minimize anti-woman abuse by reinterpreting it as an ineffectual attempt to meet a normal human need, such as intimacy or mastery (Avis, 1991, p. 10). Thus, "the majority of nonfeminist clinicians and researchers approach various forms of domestic violence . . . as symptomatic of distinct family dynamics, psychopathology and stress" (Stark & Flitcraft, 1988, p. 294). Systems theory, for example, "focuses on the processes that occur and the interrelationships between events, people, or other elements of the system," (Giles-Sims, 1983, p. 18). In a system consisting of a woman and a man, systems theory asks what circumstances precipitated the violence: Was it something the woman said or did?

Feminists reject the sociological approach as blaming the victim while ignoring the broader issues of systemic misogyny and male supremacy. Instead, they seek answers to the question of sexist violence at the group or social level, not the individual level, by attempting to understand the role of anti-woman abuse within a given society at a specific point in history (Bograd, 1988, p. 13). Feminist theorists have placed violence against women within the context of the structure of the patriarchal family (Dobash & Dobash, 1979), male supremacy (Brownmiller, 1975; Dworkin, 1981; Hanmer & Maynard, 1987), and homophobia and heterosexism (Edwards, 1987; Pharr, 1988). These concepts underscore the workings of a dominant ideology that gives men the right to control—and punish—women.

Shelley Bannister (1991) attributes the level of violence against women in society to a war fueled by misogyny that men are waging against women. According to Anne Edwards (1987), physical violence is a crucial weapon in this war: "Patriarchy or the sex/gender order as a social system concerned with the control of women has at its disposal a whole range of technique and mechanisms of control. Among these are force and physical violence" (p. 24).

Suzanne Pharr (1988) insists that men "physically and emotionally abuse women because they can, because they live in a world that gives them permission" (p. 14). Male violence, she adds, is based on men's belief that they have a right to dominate and control women, whom they view as inferior because of their gender. The result of this systemic misogyny is that the brutalization of women by men is neither accidental nor random but intentional, goal oriented, and calculated, "the heritage of a patriarchal society" (Fortune, 1990, p. 1).

Women, Violence, and News

Only within the past 15 years have researchers combined feminist theory about violence against women with studies of news coverage. For the most part, their studies have focused on rape and other sex crimes rather than on battering and other nonsexual acts of violence.

Studies of rape coverage represent the most common research involving news of violence against women. These studies have compared crime statistics with rape coverage to show that the news downplays the extent of the crime through underreporting and distorts what is reported through the omission of significant details (Lemert, 1989). Rape coverage has been found to be highly selective, portraying "a 'reality' that differed from police reports" (Schwengels & Lemert, 1986, p. 42). Rape stories also have been found to have fewer details than do stories about murder or assault (Heath, Gordon, & LeBailly, 1981).

News coverage of rape "enhances women's fears and leaves misleading impressions of both the crime and how it might be dealt with" (Gordon & Riger, 1989, p. 132). For example, potential victims could wrongly surmise from news reports that rapes occur only in dangerous parts of town and not at home. More responsible treatment by the press, these studies suggest, could dispel myths about the victim, location of the assault, and the victim's relationship with her assailant.

Discursive analyses of rape coverage also indicate that the news reinforces dominant preconceptions about women, men, and sexual violence. For example, a study of the news surrounding the rape trial of six Portuguese men in New Bedford, Massachusetts, concluded that coverage may have "narrowed the interpretive framework for understanding the crime" through its focus on legal aspects of the trial (Bumiller, 1990, p. 130). Another study of the same gang rape explored how media portrayals helped exonerate the rapists while focusing the anger of New Bedford's Portuguese community on the rape victim (Chancer, 1987).

Helen Benedict (1992) points to eight factors that lead the public and the press to blame the victims of sex crimes. Among those factors is whether the victim in any way deviated from the traditional female role of staying home with her children. Other factors include whether (a) she knew the assailant, (b) no weapon was used, (c) she was of the same race as the assailant, (d) she was of the same class as the assailant, (e) she was of the same ethnic group as the assailant, (f) she was young (although not a child), and (g) she was "pretty."

In addition, Geraldine Finn's (1989-1990) study of news coverage of "domestic terrorism" concluded that the State and the media collude to exonerate male perpetrators. She states that the inequalities of social relations "encourage and condone" violence against women and children (p. 381). Susan Edwards (1987) likewise asserts that the State has a vested interest in supporting patriarchy and is responsible for reinforcing the "acquiescence, passivity, total conformity and subjugation of women to men" as well as their acceptance of "the appropriate gender role," through its treatment of female victims of male violence (p. 152).

Gender, Race, and Class

The articulation of gender, like that of race, is a site of struggle so that a number of competing meanings are possible at any given time. It is not possible to understand gender as distinct from race or class, for all women are encoded not simply as female but also by race and other signifiers of domination and subordination. In the same manner, it is impossible to understand race or class without acknowledging the role of gender. As Elizabeth Spelman (1988) has noted, it is never the case that "the treatment of a woman has only to do with her gender and nothing to do with her class or race" (p. 53).

Stuart Hall (1981) emphasizes that the media play a key role in defining not simply what race is but also "the meaning the imagery of race carries, and what the 'problem of race' is understood to be" (p. 35). Hall links "inferential racism" with unquestioned assumptions that "enable racist statements to be formulated without ever bringing into awareness the racist predicates on which the statements are grounded" (p. 36). For example, he explains, television programs that deal with racial matters may be well-intentioned, but often they are "predicated on the unstated and unrecognized assumption that the blacks are the source of the problem" (p. 37).

Paul Gilroy (1987) maintains that "the definitive characteristic of contemporary racism is its capacity first to define blacks in the problem/victim couplet and then expel them from historical being altogether" (p. 26). Although Gilroy is writing specifically about the experience of race and racism in Britain, the cultural legacy of empire corresponds in numerous ways with the legacy of slavery in the United States. Indeed, in his description of racism, slavery and the residents of the United States can be substituted for empire and Britons:

> Racism is not a unitary event based on psychological aberration nor some ahistorical antipathy to blacks which is the cultural legacy of empire and which continues to saturate the consciousness of all white Britons regardless of age, gender, income or circumstances. It must be understood as a process. (p. 27)

Complicating the multiplicity of meanings with which race is understood is the issue of class, which is neither reducible to nor identical with race, even, as Gilroy (1987) points out, "where they become mutually entangled" (p. 40). Hall (1986) has tied class ideology to liberalism, which favors a "meritocratic society" in which energetic and enterprising individuals are presumed able to transcend their humble beginnings to reap the rewards of hard work and resourcefulness (p. 39). Hall also identifies liberalism with a free market ideology that opposes intervention by the State to remedy inequities in the distribution of resources and opportunities among competing classes (p. 41). Within liberalism, inequality and class differences appear to be the natural, commonsense outcome of initiative or lack thereof.

Because the meaning of race is never genderless, it is comprehended through consensual notions of what properly constitutes masculinity or femininity. Indeed, it is impossible to understand violence against women without understanding how race, class, and gender are intertwined within its representation. Nancy Matthews (1993) states that long before the women's movement turned its attention to the issue of rape in the 1970s, race and rape were linked during the Reconstruction Era through the lynching of black men charged with the rape of white women. The myth of the black rapist, Matthews points out, has since permeated U.S. culture and serves to keep black men and white women in their places (p. 178).

Nell Irwin Painter (1992) also points out that "the imagery of sex in race has not and does not work in identical ways for black women and men" (p. 207). Gender, race, and class are inextricably inter-woven in ways that draw on common stereotypes, with sex the "main theme associated with poverty and with blackness" (Painter, 1992, p. 206). The very term *black women* is overlaid with popular notions about just who black women are socially, politically, and economically:

> Categories like "black woman," "black women," or particular subsets of those categories, like "welfare mother/queen," are not simply social taxonomies, they are also recognized by the national public as stories that describe the world in particular and politically loaded ways—and that is exactly why they are constructed, reconstructed, manipulated and contested. (Lubiano, 1992, p. 330)

Angela Davis (1981) notes that the myth of the black woman as "chronically promiscuous" is inseparable from the myth of the black man as rapist, for if black men are invested with animal-like sexual urges, black women likewise must be invested with bestiality. The result, Davis says, is that because black women are viewed as "loose women" and whores, they are not considered legitimate victims of sexual violence (p. 182). Davis (1989) also emphasizes that rape is directly related to all the power structures in society, "reflecting the interconnectedness of the race, gender and class oppression that characterize the society" (p. 47) so that the same social conditions that spawn racist violence are also to blame for sexual violence.

Patricia Hill Collins (1993) states that racial and class inequalities are sexualized in the image of black womanhood, with race becom-ing "the distinguishing feature in determining the type of objectifi-cation women will encounter" (p. 93). White women may be depicted as objects, she states, whereas black women are depicted as animals. Thus, black women who are raped are twice victimized—first by the rape and then by society:

> Black women are more likely to be victimized than white women. Black women are less likely to report their rapes, less likely to have their cases come to trial, less likely to have their trials result in convictions, and, most disturbing, less likely to seek counseling and other support serv-ices. (p. 101)

The image of the hypersexualized black female was successfully used against Anita Hill by Senate Republicans and others intent on discrediting her charges of sexual harassment during the confirmation hearings of Supreme Court Justice Clarence Thomas (John Fiske, 1994). The durability and strength of the image of the hypersexualized black woman depend on its inverse within the popular white imagination: that of the innocent and chaste white woman.

> In American iconography, the sexually promiscuous black girl—or more precisely, the yellow girl—represents the mirror image of the white woman on the pedestal. Together, white and black women stand for woman as madonna and as whore. (Painter, 1992, p. 207)

The sexually promiscuous black woman is not, of course, the only stereotype with which African American women have been labeled. But the "oversexed-black-Jezebel," Painter (1992) states, along with the mammy and the welfare cheat, are the only roles available to black women (p. 210). Those who cannot be fit into those roles, she adds, are made to disappear from public discourse.[1]

The intersecting of the assumptions, stereotypes, and social notions embedded within cultural understandings of gender, race, class, age, and other signifiers of inequality delimits how a particular incident of violence will be portrayed within the news. One cannot assume, for example, that a black woman who is the victim of violence will be portrayed the same as a white woman who has been similarly victimized, any more than one can assume that a rich, white woman will be depicted in a manner similar to a poor, white woman or a rich African American woman to a poor African American woman.

Helen Benedict's (1992) study of sex crimes in the news found that racism and class prejudice are inherent in sex crime coverage, with crimes against white victims more likely to be covered than crimes against blacks, and black-against-white rapes covered with "exaggerated frequency, class prejudice and racist stereotypes" (p. 251). Along the same lines, Kathleen Ferraro (1993) notes that police are more likely to arrest a low-income person of color for crimes committed against a wealthy white person than they are to arrest the same person for similar offenses committed against a person of the same race and class (p. 169).

The representation of African American women who are the victims of violence occurs within the convergence of white supremacist and male supremacist ideologies. bell hooks (1992) emphasizes that this convergence is institutionalized within the mass media:

> There is a direct and abiding connection between the maintenance of white supremacist patriarchy in this society and the institutionalization via mass media of specific images, representations of race, of blackness that support and maintain the oppression, exploitation, and overall domination of all black people. (p. 2)

Indeed, the presumption of guilt, always there for women, applies even more so to black women. Ann Jones (1980) notes that whereas middle-class, white women are discriminated against within the legal system, poor women of color are even less likely to be treated fairly. Carole Sheffield (1987) also points out that "the good woman/bad woman dichotomy has particularly troublesome consequences for black women in our society" because black women are seen as inherently inferior and, therefore, can never achieve goodness (p. 173). As bell hooks (1992) explains in an essay that examines the representation of the singer Madonna and her appropriation of black culture,

> The socially constructed image of innocent white womanhood relies on the continued production of the racist/sexist sexual myth that black women are not innocent and never can be. Since we are coded always as "fallen" women in the racist cultural iconography we can never, as can Madonna, publicly "work" the image of ourselves as innocent female daring to be bad. Mainstream culture always reads the black female body as sign of sexual experience. . . . the very image of sexual agency that she [Madonna] is able to project and affirm with material gain has been the stick this society has used to justify its continued beating and assault on the black female body. (pp. 159-160)

Although feminists have theorized the relationship between gender and race, studies that have focused primarily on the representation of race within the news have not addressed the convergence of multiple oppressions. Research into racial representation within the news has, for the most part, ignored women of color. A rare exception is Jo Ellen Fair's (1993) study of U.S. television news stories of violence among blacks in South Africa. She found that racialization, as part of the ideological process of classification and marginalization, combined with gender labeling to further marginalize and silence black South African women.

More typically, studies that have examined race within the news have concluded that the news is structured by and reinforces racial ideology, the result of which is that blacks, and black youths in particular (Hall et al., 1978), are represented as a problem and threat to society (Entman, 1990, 1992; Gray, 1989; Hall et al., 1978; Hartmann & Husband, 1974; Shah & Thornton, 1994; van Dijk, 1991). Teun van Dijk (1991) claims that the news reflects "elite racism" because elites are most able to use the media to reproduce and reinforce a white, ethnic consensus that most benefits themselves.

Robert Entman (1990) also suggests that "the emphasis and portrayal of crime in local TV news stimulates whites' animosity toward blacks" (p. 332). He found that "modern racism" in television news places African Americans outside "the symbolic boundaries of the community" by portraying them as more threatening as criminals and more practiced in special interests as politicians than their white counterparts (p. 342).

Although these studies found that the news reflected and reinforced racial biases and stereotypes in its representation of race, their primary—albeit unstated—focus was the portrayal of black men. These studies did not address the place of women of color within the news, presumably assuming that gender distinction was unimportant. Nor did they explore the representation of violence against women of color. In addition, the question of class was subsumed within the representation of race in these studies so that class appeared primarily in the context of stereotypes concerning African Americans.[2]

Battered Women and Self-Defense

This chapter will conclude with a look at the ways in which the mythology of anti-woman violence is embedded within and affects the legal system as it deals with battered women who kill their abusers in self-defense. An examination of how these women are treated by the judiciary is particularly useful in examining the legal system's and society's responses to women who step outside the traditional role of victim. It also illustrates how the mythology of anti-woman violence is "naturalized" within the legal system and the consequences of this for women who fight back. As Kathleen Ferraro (1993) notes, the goal of the criminal justice system is to protect and reinforce the existing social order through the punishment of individuals who are seen to be deviant as a result of pathological psyches (p. 165). This is fundamentally at odds with a feminist analysis that "views male violence as an expression of class, race, gender and heterosexual privilege" (p. 165). Ferraro also points out that police and other workers in the criminal justice system view battering as gender neutral, as a problem of dysfunctional or pathological families.

The numbers, however, belie gender neutrality. Men are far more likely to be violent, both in their relationships with wives and girlfriends and with other men. For example, men commit two thirds of intraspousal homicides, although fewer than 6% of men in state prisons were there for killing a relative or intimate. In contrast, more than 25% of the women incarcerated for violent crimes were convicted of killing a family member, former spouse, or other intimate (Bannister, 1991, p. 406). Often, these women were defending themselves from abuse (Browne, 1987; Stout, 1991; Walker, 1989). In 1987, 800 women were incarcerated for killing their male partners (Reynolds, 1987, as cited in Stout, 1991, p. 9).

One study found that half the battered women incarcerated for murdering their abusers were given life sentences without the possibility of parole (Stout, 1991, p. 19). Battered and raped women are frequently denied justice because "the prevailing standard of justice is male," with discriminatory laws and discriminatory discretion exercised by police, prosecutors, judges, and jurors (Jones, 1980, p. 310). This is particularly true for women who kill their abusers in self-defense. These women, according to Ann Jones (1980), are "deprived at every step of equal protection under the law; and even those women who receive fair and equal treatment are likely to be thought of as having gotten away with something" (p. 311).

Lenore Walker (1989) explains that battered women who kill their abusers are unfairly judged because of the marginal status of women in society:

This marginal position is one reason why women, like minorities and other oppressed groups in any society, are judged harshly when they strike back at a powerful oppressor. And if average, everyday "normal" women are judged harshly, women considered to fall outside the norms of acceptable female behavior (whether emotionally, occupationally, or otherwise) are likely to be judged even more unfairly. (p. 237)

Women who kill their batterers generally face harsh sentences, even though many had endured years of unspeakable torture and abuse before the final battering incident that resulted in the death of their abusers. Karen Stout (1991) states that "the majority of women imprisoned for homicide were battered by the men they killed, and the violence against them had escalated in severity and prevalence over time" (p. 11). Charles Ewing (1987) also points out that "many battered women who kill and plead self-defense are convicted of murder or manslaughter despite abundant evidence that they were severely abused, both physically and psychologically, by the men they eventually killed" (p. 46). One study of 30 women incarcerated for murder found that 29 had been battered and that 20 had been trying to protect themselves or their children when the murder occurred (Totman, 1978). Lenore Walker (1989) also found that 76% of the women whose murder weapon was a gun had been threatened with use of that gun by their male partners.

Shelley Bannister (1991) maintains that battered women who have been incarcerated for acts of self-defense against their male abusers are political prisoners, deserving of the same protection under international law as other political prisoners in the United States (p. 401). A woman who successfully defends herself against her abuser by killing him or causing serious bodily injury, she states, is striking a blow against all men and the State, which has not simply failed to protect her but is instrumental in maintaining the system of oppression that subordinates women (p. 410). Bannister adds that women who kill their abusers are incarcerated by the State for several reasons:

1) to deter other women from believing that they can similarly resist; 2) to reinforce in women the belief that they have no right to their own bodies' integrity and no right to defend against or resist male attacks; and, 3) to assert and protect men's power over women. (p. 410)

Generally, women charged with killing their batterers plead either insanity or self-defense. The insanity defense, which is rarely used, inappropriately labels the woman as crazy for fighting back and well may "result in her being committed to a mental institution for a far longer time and under far worse conditions than if she had been convicted of a crime and sent to prison" (Gillespie, 1989, p. 25).

The self-defense plea usually involves testimony that the woman suffered from what Walker (1984) has called the "battered woman syndrome." The syndrome involves a three-stage cycle of violence in which (a) tension builds and abuse is considered minor, (b) the acute battering incident occurs and the woman is severely beaten, and (c) the battering stops and the man appears contrite and seeks forgiveness. The violence escalates as the cycle is repeated so that the beatings become progressively more severe and more frequent.

Most battered women who kill their abusers are convicted due to the narrow confines of the law of self-defense and the "deadly force doctrine," which stipulates that deadly force is not justified as self-defense unless it reasonably appeared necessary as a way for the woman to protect herself from imminent death or serious bodily injury (Ewing, 1987; Gillespie, 1989). The fact that the woman had survived previous batterings is used against her, for juries question how a woman reasonably could have concluded that she was in imminent danger when she had survived previous beatings without being killed.

Similarly, the woman's continued existence allows police, judges, juries, and attorneys to question whether she used excessive force. Ferraro (1993) states that the legal terms *probable cause, fault,* and *harm* require women to demonstrate clearly and consistently "that they have been severely injured, have not fought back with greater violence than they received, and do want their abusers arrested and prosecuted" (p. 174). When a woman's act of self-defense results in the death of her abuser, she is assumed to have used greater violence. This, of course, ignores the reality that, because the vast majority of men are physically stronger than women, the playing ground is uneven. For a woman to defend herself from being beaten to death, it is often necessary for her to use a gun or knife rather than rely on her own physical power.

The law of self-defense, Ewing (1987) maintains, also "does not give adequate consideration to the awful psychological plight of the battered woman or to the possibility that, under certain circumstances, killing her batterer to escape that plight may be an entirely reasonable and justifiable act" (p. 59). Ewing argues that women kill in "psychological self-defense" to prevent their batterers from destroying their psychological selves.

Cynthia Gillespie (1989) states that the "law of self-defense is a law for men" based on assumptions related to men fighting men (p. 4). Those assumptions include the notion that the two adversaries are roughly equivalent in size and strength, that it is unmanly to kill an unarmed person, and that hands and feet—which batterers frequently use to pummel and even kill women—are not serious threats. The law also assumes that antagonists are strangers or perhaps acquaintances who have a safe place to which they can retreat or escape.

Gillespie claims the interaction of the law of self-defense and social bias—which appears in the attitudes of the police, prosecuting attorneys, judges, and juries—results in a double standard because women are convicted for acts with which men would never have been charged. This interaction between law and social bias, she adds, "works to deprive most women of any effective right to self-defense at all" (p. 30).

The law of self-defense also illustrates the interconnection of gender, race, and class in the mythology of anti-woman violence:

> In fact, the success of the self-defense argument often rests not on the facts of the case but on the color of the "criminal." . . . Black women have less claim to self-defense because in the eyes of white jurors they are not real "ladies" whom men should refrain from hitting. . . . the black women who kills in self-defense is likely to be seen as just another violent black person, shooting it out. . . . Ironically, the criminal justice system, which often is eager to believe that black men are naturally violent and threatening, is willing to give them the benefit of the doubt only when the people they attack are their black wives and girl friends. (Jones, 1980, p. 316)

Although feminists have examined the criminal justice system's response to battered women who kill, news coverage of women who defend themselves against male violence has not previously been studied. Carol Gardner (1990) conducted research that is probably closest to this topic when she examined popular literature—primarily women's magazines and how-to books—concerning women and self-defense. She found that the rhetoric of popular literature concerning women's self-defense in public places "imputes limited competence" for women and "connotes ineptness rather than skill, apprehension rather than ability, a self debased rather than revered" (p. 312). The rhetoric of limited competence "communicates dependency and lack of skill" (p. 316) and is based on judgments of appearance:

> Those who seek to escape victimization must depend on assessment of strangers' appearance and manipulation of their own in order to avoid crime. One way to cope with crime in public therefore will be to develop an array of behavioral strategies that are also appearance dependent. (p. 314)

Those behavioral strategies include not being alone—or seeming to be alone—in public, walking in the middle of the street at night, manipulating dress and behavior so as not to appear attractive, carrying money in the bra, walking with a whistle in the mouth, and always remaining ever vigilant. Taken as a whole, the strategies—and the popular literature that promotes them—not only offer guidance to women who seek to remain safe but also provide a warning about the possible repercussions for those who would ignore them. "Good girls," the popular literature implies, follow the rules and, in doing so, stay out of trouble; "bad girls" do not follow the rules and, therefore, get what they deserve. As the following chapters demonstrate, news coverage of violence against women follows a similar pattern.

Notes

1. Lubiano (1992) notes the existence of the stereotype of the overachieving "black lady," who can be blamed for the demoralization and betrayal of black males.

2. For example, Gray (1989) concluded that news coverage attributes the black "underclass" to individual shortcomings, and Entman (1992) suggests that poor blacks "signify a social menace that must be contained" (p. 378).

CHAPTER
3

The Murder
of a Battered Woman

On the night of August 9, 1990, Wanda Walters, who had moved out of the suburban Atlanta home she had shared with her husband Dennis, returned to pick up her remaining possessions. Heated words were exchanged, and Dennis retreated into the bedroom. When he reemerged, he was carrying a Colt revolver. Wanda was outside in the driveway, next to the car in which she had arrived. Dennis shot Wanda four times in the back and then shot himself in the head. She died instantly; he died 24 hours later in a hospital.

Wanda was the 12th of 14 children born to Louvale Westbrooks. The news made much of the family's poverty, noting that Louvale had gone to churches asking for food, clothing, and money when her children were young. When Wanda was 14, she became sexually involved with Dennis, who was 23 years her senior and married to his third wife. Dennis and his wife then adopted Wanda, and Dennis later divorced his wife, signed away his adoption rights, and married Wanda.

News coverage of Wanda's murder was extensive and in-depth—the result of Dennis's high profile as director of Atlanta's Cyclorama, a popular tourist attraction that depicts the Civil War's Battle of Atlanta, and the fact that Dennis had fought, and won, a reverse discrimination lawsuit against the city for the Cyclorama position. In addition, the in-depth coverage may have been a result of the unusual circumstances of the relationship between Wanda and Dennis.

Two articles appeared in the *Atlanta Journal/Constitution* about the murder of Wanda Walters. The first article, written by Katie Long, appeared in the morning *Atlanta Constitution* on August 11, 1990. The second, written by Gary Pomerantz, appeared in the Sunday *Atlanta Journal/Constitution* on September 9, 1990. (See Appendix on pp. 127-133.) This chapter provides a close textual analysis of those articles. The news stories indicate that coverage of violence against women reflects myths, stereotypes, and assumptions rooted in patriarchal ideology. The coverage places anti-woman violence within the context of individual and family pathology rather than attributing it to social structures and socially approved gender roles. In doing this, the news denied that Wanda Walters was, in fact, abused. At the same time, it absolved her husband of responsibility for his actions. In addition, the analysis demonstrates the interconnection of gender, race, and class in the representation of sexist violence.

The Story in Pictures

The two articles about the murder of Wanda Walters were prominently displayed—particularly the follow-up. The first story began on the front page of the metropolitan-state news section of the newspaper. Its jump[1] contained two photos—one was a head shot of Dennis Walters, which noted he "Sued city to get Cyclorama job," and the other was of the suburban home that was the "crime scene."

The second story was an in-depth feature that attempted to explain how the murder came about. It began at the top of the front page of the Sunday paper, where it covered five of the newspaper's six columns and included a photo of Dennis and Wanda in 1986 "as father and daughter." The jump took up almost a full page and contained four more pictures. A small insert of the couple "as man and wife" was in the middle of the page, and two photos of Dennis in a professional capacity were at the bottom. The representations of Wanda and Dennis in the photos in both stories emphasize her dependence on him for definition and his independence through his work. There are no photos of Wanda other than those defining her role as "wife" to Dennis's "man" (not husband) or as "daughter" to his "father."

The largest and most prominent photo (see Photo 3.1), at the top of the jump page, was of Wanda's mother, Louvale Westbrooks—slouched in a torn, reclining chair, overweight and barefoot, a grandchild at her feet. In this photo, a floor lamp with neither bulb nor shade is near a porch door propped open by what appears to be a ceiling light fixture. The cinder block wall behind the door appears dirty. The cutline, echoing a theme within the story, informs the reader that she "caught Dennis Walters and her 14-year-old daughter having sex."

The convergence of class, gender, and race in this photo and cutline signify Wanda's mother not simply as a poor, white woman but as a poor, white woman unable or unwilling to care about her appearance or to exert moral control over her young daughter. Within the historically distinct race, class, and gender consciousness of the South, she is made to signify what many Southerners, black and white, disdain as "white trash."[2] In this way, Wanda is defined not only by her relationship to Dennis but by her relationship to her mother. If her mother is "trash," so, then, is she.

Obsession as Pathology

In the stories, Dennis's mental state is used to explain why he killed Wanda and then himself. The first story merely quotes a police officer's opinion that Dennis Walters apparently "was having an extremely difficult time dealing with" his separation from Wanda. However, from the first sentence of the second article—"Dennis Walters was a man of obsessions"—his emotional and mental health are framed as obsessive and are represented as the cause of his

Photo 3.1. The mother of Warda Cosper, Louvale Westbrooks—shown here with a grandchild—caught Dennis Walters and her 14-year-old daughter having sex.

Printed courtesy of the Atlanta Journal Constitution and by permission of photographer Nick Arroyo.

actions: Dennis "used a blue-steel Colt revolver to fight his personal obsession"; Wanda's first attempt to leave him "fell prey to Dennis Walters's obsession" when he broke down the door to her apartment, beat her, and took her home with him.

Dennis also "brooded" over the impending divorce and Wanda's new boyfriend, and he "fumed" about her staying out late—or all night—in the months prior to their separation. His brother is quoted as saying he believed Dennis "ultimately was broken by the notion of having lost his wife to another man" and that he "was not of sound mind" six weeks before the murder when he wrote a will that alluded to what was to come and requested a double funeral. Drawing on a deposition from the reverse discrimination lawsuit against the city, the article even quotes then-Mayor Andrew Young calling Dennis "a nut." Dennis's mental condition on the night of the murder is of particular concern: Dennis had been drinking, heated words were exchanged, and "something snapped," causing Dennis to go into the house for a gun with which to shoot Wanda and then himself.

The notion that "something snapped" implies a spontaneous reaction, a spur-of-the-moment, uncontrollable response. This belies the fact that Wanda's murder was planned at least six weeks earlier, when Dennis wrote his will. The representation of Dennis as obsessed or out of control offers both a rationale and an excuse for his actions. As a pathological individual, a victim of his own obsession, he is not responsible for his behavior. Even the statement that Dennis "apparently had planned the tragedy"—not the murder, but the "tragedy"—denies his responsibility. Tragedy does not happen to the perpetrators of crimes. To characterize what happened as a tragedy is to represent Dennis Walters as a victim, just as Wanda was.

As yet another indication of his mental state, and what the newspaper characterized as Dennis's ability to be "headstrong" with Wanda, the feature story notes that Dennis "had played Russian roulette with her, pointing a gun at her head and clicking the trigger." Wanda's brother explains Dennis's actions by recounting what Dennis told him: There was a dud bullet in the gun, and Dennis was merely testing Wanda's "toughness." However, the term *Russian roulette* generally assumes a voluntary "game" of reciprocal bravado in which participants spin a gun, with one cartridge in it, on its side until it comes to a stop. The person it points to then puts the gun to her or his own head and pulls the trigger. There is no indication that Wanda agreed to have a gun put to her head or that Dennis participated in the game as a potential target. By referring to Dennis's actions as "playing" Russian roulette, the article denies the seriousness of what was essentially an act of terrorization and domination.

Blaming the Victim

In addition, by representing Dennis's obsession as the reason for his actions, Wanda becomes the only one who is in control of the situation. If she let it get out of hand, then, she has no one but herself to blame. This blaming of the victim "diverts attention from the true abuser or the cause of the victimization" (Pharr, 1988, p. 60) and becomes a primary barrier to social change (Ryan, 1971).

The news codes of "objectivity" and "balance"—of "getting both sides of the story"—also negate the seriousness of the crime and represent Wanda as at least partly at fault. The first article notes the conditions surrounding the shooting: Dennis "had been drinking" when Wanda stopped by for her belongings, and an "argument erupted." Although this implicates alcohol and, by extension, Dennis, it also exonerates him because he was, presumably, under the influence. The use of the passive voice here also eliminates human agency so that it is not clear from the article who started the argument.

But the follow-up article is quite specific in pointing to provocations by Wanda who, like Dennis, is characterized as "headstrong and prone to jealousy." After detailing how Dennis would "test" Wanda's "toughness" with Russian roulette, the article attempts to achieve balance by noting that Wanda "could test her husband's toughness in other ways." She wore "the fancy dresses her husband had purchased for their social events" when she "left alone for the evening for an unannounced destination" from which she returned after midnight. Occasionally, the article added, Wanda even "stopped at her husband's home at 6 a.m. to shower" before going to work. She also is reported to have "playfully" suggested to her estranged husband that perhaps they could begin to date again after the divorce. And she was "wearing his mother's diamond-studded necklace" when she arrived to pick up her belongings the night she was murdered. Wanda's choice of clothing and jewelry is presented as equivalent to Dennis's pointing a gun to her head and pulling the trigger. Both actions are represented as ways they tested each other's toughness, although Wanda's also signifies as provocation.

Behind the representation of Wanda's attire as attempts to provoke Dennis is the notion that he had a right to determine what she wore, that he was entitled to control Wanda's choice of clothing and, by extension, her body. The signification of women's clothing and bodies as provocation is central to the belief that a woman causes her own victimization by what she wears, how she sits, and where and when she goes out.

Wanda's background is offered as a plausible explanation for why a 14-year-old would become sexually involved with a married man and threaten to disown her mother if she didn't consent to her adoption by him. Wanda is represented as using Dennis as her way out of the poverty into which she was born. Indeed, the only explanation for why Wanda stayed and what she got out of the relationship is in the lengthy treatment of her background and family. Wanda was, the article states, "the 12th of 14 children from a broken family . . . that long has remained in the grips of poverty."

Details about Louvale Westbrooks's past and current home situation—no telephone, no running water for the first six months of the year, 5 of 14 children taken by the state in 1957—reinforce the white trash stereotype while stigmatizing poor women as inadequate. The notion of Wanda as being—or coming from—white trash is supported with the anecdote that, during arguments, Dennis would offer to build her a "little white-trash room" where, he would tell her, she could go when she wanted to act like her family. The contrast between Wanda's background and Dennis's "solidly middle-class family" also is reinforced in the feature by interviews with her siblings—who recall their parents in soup lines and asking for food, money, and clothing at churches—and by the prominently displayed photo of her mother. In this way, the symbolic representations of class, race, and gender within the newspaper's photos work intertextually with the stories.

Neither of the articles mentions Wanda's feelings for or about Dennis at any time during their years together, although the second story goes to great lengths to emphasize Dennis's love and obsession for Wanda. Indeed, the message that Dennis murdered Wanda out of love was a constant refrain throughout the second article. The feature story headline was "Walters family affair: A fatal attraction." A subordinate headline, or deck, quoted Dennis as saying, "I never loved anybody like that girl. . . . Never like this." This quote was from the story, in which Dennis's brother recalls Dennis's telling him, " 'I've never loved anybody like that girl. I thought I'd been in love before, but never like this.' " The banner headline on the jump page was more explicit: "Walters: In the end, his love consumed them both."

But Dennis Walters was not just a victim of his obsession and love for Wanda. The first two paragraphs of the feature indicate that Dennis was *Wanda's* victim: "Nothing owned his spirit like the Civil War and his fourth wife, Wanda. The first was the vehicle for his rise, the latter for his fall." She was, it seems, the cause of his demise, responsible for his death as well as her own.

Although Wanda is represented as (at least partly) responsible for her own death and Dennis's, she remains symbolically unimportant. Throughout both stories, Wanda has been silenced. The headline of the first article—"Cyclorama chief tries to end life of battles"—does not even hint at his having murdered Wanda. Instead, the headline tells us Dennis Walters—and his actions—are what's important. Not until the fourth paragraph of the story—after learning that Dennis Walters "fought for years to gain his lifelong dream—the directorship of the popular Civil War tourist attraction"—does the reader learn that "Mr. Walters shot his wife four times in the back and then shot himself in the head" in the driveway of their suburban home. The headline on the jump for the first story, "Walters: Shoots wife, then himself," similarly denies Wanda's importance. It does not say, "Walters: Murdered by husband," which would make her the subject rather than the object of the story. The headline also equalizes Dennis's actions—he did to her what he did to himself. She suffered no more than he. Or as the article suggests, he may have suffered more. He was the victim of his obsessions, devastated by Wanda's leaving. She, on the other hand, had plans to remarry.

Discussion

The two articles represent Wanda's murder as an aberration, as the product of individual pathology rather than the logical result of the systematic oppression of women. This representation is similar in content to the underlying assumptions of traditional sociological studies that "not only obscure the actual history of violence against women, but by disregarding the feminist critique of patriarchy, they effectively discourage analysis of family violence from a context of both societal and male supremacy" (DeLauretis, 1987, p. 34)

Mildred Pagelow (1981) equates male domination and control of women in the home with the notion of "women as property requiring varying degrees of control, much like children, domesticated animals and pets" (p. 63). As with children and pets, a certain amount of control is deemed not only justifiable but necessary. The question then becomes not whether Wanda's murder was justified, for that would place responsibility squarely on the shoulders of her murderer, but whether she brought it on herself. At the very least, the articles suggest that her death is equivalent to Dennis's—they are represented as the same tragedy, the result of Dennis's obsessive love over which he had no control. At most, Wanda provoked Dennis and got what she deserved.

Shelley Bannister (1991) notes that batterers are rarely convicted of a criminal offense, and law enforcement officers and judges tend to be lenient when dealing with men who batter, because they frequently believe that the women provoked their abusers. An analogy can be made with Andrea Dworkin's (1981) contention that women are seen as holding sexual power over men when, in fact, men have the power of sex:

> The argument is that women have sexual power because erection is involuntary; a woman is the presumed cause; therefore, the man is helpless; the woman is powerful. The male reacts to a stimulation for which he is not responsible; it is his very nature to do so; whatever he does he does because of a provocation that inheres in the female. (p. 22)

The representation of Dennis as a victim and of Wanda's murder as obsession gone awry is incompatible with a feminist perspective that views their relationship as one of male control and female subordination and as characterized by victimization, incest, misogyny, abuse of power, domination, battering, and, ultimately, murder. The newspaper coverage denies that Dennis sought to control and, in fact, own Wanda—first through adoption and then, when she was old enough, through marriage. It even denies that Wanda was a battered woman—the terms *battered* or *battered woman* are never used, despite the fact that Dennis was reported to have beaten her in her apartment and pointed a gun to her head. To acknowledge Wanda as a battered women would have changed the context of the story and signified Dennis as an aggressor, rather than as obsessed or head-strong, and Wanda as *his* victim. As Geraldine Finn (1989-1990) points out, white, middle-class men who batter or kill their wives are

> constructed in state and media discourses as the victims of provocation or personal stress, more deserving of mercy and compassion than condemnation and constraint. (p. 381)

An alternative framing of Wanda's murder would recognize that the victimization of women is sanctioned by society, that misogyny and the oppression of women are the real reasons that men like Dennis Walters believe they have the right to control women and, when they fear they are losing control, to murder them. That Dennis Walters also killed himself should not deflect attention from this. Despite the newspaper's characterization of Wanda's death and Dennis's suicide as the same "tragedy," they are separate and moti-vated differently. Wanda did not choose to die; Dennis made that choice for her and, then, for himself.

Dennis's suicide also should not be viewed as evidence of his not being responsible for his actions. Although his reasons for taking his own life are less clear than his reasons for murdering Wanda, he may have viewed suicide as preferable to jail. What is clear is that there is no evidence that Wanda remained in an abusive relationship because she was somehow using Dennis. She did, after all, attempt to leave before—and was beaten by Dennis and taken home.

According to Del Martin (1976), women remain in abusive rela-tionships because (a) they fear what their partners might do to them if they left and were caught, (b) societal pressure to remain in a marriage is intense, and (c) they do not have the financial resources to leave (see pp. 73-87). Elizabeth Stanko (1985) states that women remain in abusive relationships "because of the real conditions of their lives within a male-dominated world. Men's power is not an individual, but a collective one. Women's lives are bounded by it" (p. 57).

The representation of Wanda as guilty of both her own murder and Dennis's suicide reflects what Martin (1976) has called "society's almost tangible contempt for female victims of violence" (p. 6). The coverage also provides evidence of an ethical double standard. Besides murder, Dennis is guilty of incest, adultery, and statutory rape. This is not the sort of man one would expect to receive sympathetic news coverage. Yet Dennis's "moral lapses" are excused, whereas Wanda is blamed for her own murder (and Dennis's death) because of what she wore, how late she stayed out, and her family's background. In this way, the discursive representation of gender, race, and class converged in a multiplicity of oppression that marked Wanda as "guilty."

Violence against women must be understood within a complexity of oppression that victimizes women not simply because of their sex but because the symbolic representation of gender is inextricably tied to issues of race and class. As Sandra Bartky (1990) explains,

> All the modes of oppression—psychological, political, economic—and the kinds of alienation they generate serve to maintain a vast system of privilege—privilege of race, of sex, and of class. Each mode of oppression within the system has its own part to play, but each serves to support and maintain the others. (p. 32)

In Wanda's case, race and class were conflated in the signifier "white trash." For a middle-class black woman—or any other woman—gender, race, and class are no less intertwined. However, "the interlocking character of the modes of oppression" (Bartky, 1990, p. 32) is not limited to sexism, racism, and classism but includes ageism, heterosexism, and any number of other signifiers of domination and exclusion.

In applying feminist theory to the textual analysis of news coverage of Wanda Walters's murder, this study discloses the underlying assumptions, myths, and stereotypes that shaped that coverage. The news, socially constructed, represents the values of the dominant social order (Gans, 1980; Roshco, 1975). Because that order is steeped in an ethic of male supremacy, the news reflects this. By perpetuating the idea that violence against women is a problem of individual pathology, the news disguises the social roots of battering while reinforcing stereotypes and myths that blame women. In this way, the news sustains and reproduces male supremacy.

Notes

1. A jump is the continuation of a story on a different page.

2. *The Encyclopedia of Southern Culture* (1989) notes that the term *poor white* has "connotations of moral as well as material impoverishment and even degeneracy" and, in the antebellum period, was used to describe "the character of a people, rather than strictly being a term of economic classification" (p. 1405). The myth of "poor, white trash" characterized poor Appalachians as "backward hillbillies who were inclined toward incest, fundamentalist religion, laziness and irresponsibility" (p. 1138).

C H A P T E R
4

Good Girls, Bad Girls, and TV News

When network television news covers incidents of violence against women, the stories more often than not are sensationalized and involve either celebrities or what is considered a particularly gruesome or unusual case. The rape trials of boxer Mike Tyson and Kennedy family member William Kennedy Smith, as well as the murder trial of former football star and Grade B movie actor O. J. Simpson, who was charged with and acquitted of killing his ex-wife and her friend, fall into the former category. Coverage of the attack on the so-called Central Park Jogger and of the gang rape of a woman in a bar in New Bedford, Massachusetts, are examples of the latter.

However, none of these stories reflects the common, less sensationalized violence experienced in staggering numbers by women every day. This routine, more typical violence is far more likely to be covered by local television than by network news, although local news covers only a fraction of the sexist violence that exists in any community.

Just how local television news covers violence against women is important not simply because local news helps shape a community's perceptions and awareness of safety and crime within its midst but also because such coverage can influence public policy (Loseke, 1989). If violence against women is represented as an affront to society and as the serious social problem that it is, public officials may be more likely to pass laws to curb anti-woman violence, and law enforcement and judicial personnel may be more inclined to treat violators like the criminals they are.

This study examined local television news coverage of violence against women through content analysis and textual analysis. The content analysis provided a framework for understanding the broad parameters in which television news represents women who are the victims of violence; the textual analysis then probed the underlying ideology within the news.

Close analysis revealed that the news, in keeping with the virgin-whore or good girl-bad girl dichotomy, divides female victims of male violence into innocent victims or women who are guilty of causing or provoking their own suffering. The findings also suggest that news coverage of violence against women serves as a warning to women by defining the boundaries of appropriate behavior and the punishment for transgression. The analysis shows how race, class, and age are inextricably linked to gender in the representation of sexist violence.

The 11 p.m. 30-minute newscasts[1] from the ABC, NBC, and CBS network affiliates in Atlanta, Georgia (WSB, WXIA, and WAGA, respectively[2]), were taped for 7.5 weeks—for 53 days beginning June 30 and ending August 21, 1991—and then coded.[3]

Each instance of violence against a woman or women was coded for primary type of violence (murder, rape, battering by partner, beating by nonpartner, kidnapping, and other),[4] race of both assailant and victim, sex of assailant, number of victims and assailants, age of primary victim, social class[5] of victim and assailant, and context of coverage (whether the story resulted from the coverage of police, the courts, reporter initiative, or other).[6] Overall intercoder agreement was 90.5% and ranged from 80% to 100%.[7]

Table 4.1 Primary Type of Violence and Victim, by Percentage

Type of violence	
Murder	36.6
Rape	28.3
Battering (by partner)	5.4
Beating (by nonpartner)	2.4
Kidnapping	4.4
Other	22.9
Primary victim	
Adult	56.6
Child	15.1
Teenager	9.8
Elderly	11.7
Unknown	6.8

Findings

In all, 205 stories involving violence against one or more women were coded. Murder was the most common primary violence reported, accounting for 36.6% ($n = 75$) of the total number of stories. The second most common primary violence was rape, with 28.3% ($n = 58$) of the total. In 62.4% ($n = 128$) of the stories, only one victim was involved, and in 79.5% ($n = 163$), there was only one assailant. Most victims, 56.6% ($n = 116$), were adults ranging in age from 20 to 64 years, although 24.9% ($n = 51$) were either children or teenagers, and 11.7% ($n = 24$) were 65 years of age or older (see Table 4.1).

Although the race of the victim was not identified 62% ($n = 127$) of the time, in 24.9% ($n = 51$) of the stories, the victim was white, and in 11.2% ($n = 23$), she was black.[8]

Only 2.4% ($n = 5$) of the assailants were identified as women. When the assailant was identified by race, he—or the rare she—was black in 25.9% ($n = 53$) of the stories and white in 28.3% ($n = 58$). The vast majority of both assailants and victims could not be identified by class. When they could, however, the largest category for both was upper-middle class/wealthy. The study found that 20% ($n = 41$) of the assailants, when identifiable, were either middle class/professional or upper-middle class/wealthy, and 15.1% ($n = 31$) of the victims could be classified as such. In contrast, only 3.4% ($n = 7$) of

Good Girls, Bad Girls, and TV News

Table 4.2 Race and Class Status of Primary Victim, by Percentage

Race	
White	24.9
Black	11.2
Other	2.0
Unknown	62.0
Class status	
Poor	1.5
Working class	3.4
Middle class/professional	7.3
Upper-middle class/wealthy	7.8
Unknown	80.0

the victims were identified as working class, and 1.5% ($n = 3$) as poor (see Table 4.2). None of the assailants was coded as poor, and only 2.9% ($n = 6$) were coded as working class. These findings are the result, most likely, of both the news media's proclivity for emphasizing the wealthy and de-emphasizing other classes and the difficulty of coding for class.

In sum, the findings indicate that more than twice as many victims were identifiable as white than as black. When both the victims and assailants were identifiable by class, most were middle class/professional or upper-middle class/wealthy. It may seem, then, that a disproportionate number of stories deal with white women who have money. Because most victims are not identified by race or class, however, that may not be the case. Nevertheless, the fact that the victim is white and has money appears to be of more news value, and therefore is more likely to be mentioned, than if the victim is poor and black.

The study also found that 63.9% ($n = 131$) of the stories were reported as the result of covering the police, and 27.8% ($n = 57$) involved pretrial or trial coverage. Only 2.9% ($n = 6$) of the stories appeared to be the result of reporter initiative, a not surprising finding given that most news is event oriented, and crime news is considered an event best covered through the police beat (see Table 4.3).

This quantitative assessment was useful in providing an outline of how local television news reported violence against women. How-

Table 4.3 Context of Coverage, by Percentage

Police	63.9
Courts	27.8
Reporter initiative	2.9
Other	5.4

ever, to get a sense of how ideology is interwoven into this coverage, it is necessary to examine the text more closely. Thirty-two stories were selected for further analysis. These stories were not chosen to be statistically representative but, rather, to illustrate the workings of ideology within the news.[9]

The textual analysis revealed patterns that polarized around the victim's presumed guilt or innocence. For the most part, women were portrayed as being either blameless in their victimization or somehow at fault and responsible for what happened to them. At issue is not the man's guilt or innocence in assaulting the woman but the woman's guilt or innocence in precipitating the attack. The stories, along with those in which blame did not appear to be at issue, serve as a warning to women by delineating the social boundaries around which guilt can be assessed.

The section that follows describes how the discourse of crime news works to portray women as innocent or guilty. More specifically, it shows how news conventions and codes work ideologically to either exonerate the victim or proclaim her guilt. The signification of a victim's guilt does not necessarily imply that she deserved the abuse, although in some extreme instances that may be the underlying assumption within the news. Rather, the implication of guilt, which most often is partial in its representation, is tied to the woman's actions so that it appears that something she has said or done precipitated, provoked, or allowed the violence to occur.

It should be emphasized that the representation of innocence is not considered problematic within the context of this study, for women who are the victims of sexist violence are, indeed, innocent. However, so are those who are made to appear guilty of somehow contributing to or allowing the abuse to occur. It is the latter representation that is both inappropriate and dangerous to women.

Innocent Victims

Women who were represented as wholly undeserving of violence and abuse were either very young or very old, had been tortured or murdered in a particularly gruesome manner, or had been attacked by a serial murderer, serial rapist, or someone characterized as mentally ill. These conditions were not mutually exclusive, and the existence of more than one of these aspects in a story virtually guaranteed its newsworthiness. For example, the murder of a child by a serial killer generated more extensive coverage than the murder of a child by her father.

The innocence of victims was established primarily through the use of videotape and graphics—artists' thematic renderings and still photographs—as well as the comments and behavior of reporters, anchors, and interviewed sources. The videotape, graphics, and comments portrayed an inequity in size and power between the victim and her attacker so that the female victim appeared vulnerable or frail, whereas her male attacker was portrayed as physically overpowering. Videotape displaying the reactions of neighbors and others also showed the audience how to react appropriately. In addition, reporter and anchor comments, as well as those of sources interviewed, provided evidence of the victim's innocence, as well as the horrific nature of the crime.

Murdered children were frequently portrayed as innocent of provoking their attack. Given social taboos concerning incest and child abuse, few people would blame a 2-year-old for having been raped and murdered by her father. Indeed, most people would be horrified, which makes the story all the more newsworthy.

One station opened its newscast with the story of a 2-year-old girl not expected to live after being "physically and sexually assaulted" by her father. The drawing of a hand about to hit a child, with the caption "child beaten," appeared behind the anchor as the evening news began. The camera then cut to the child's 21-year-old father, who is black, being led out of police headquarters to a waiting car as the reporter listed the charges against him: "molestation, cruelty to children, aggravated assault."

This was followed by footage of the outside of a brick apartment building, where the camera focused on the number above the mailbox in front of the building, as the reporter announced: "He was with his 2-year-old daughter at this East Lake Meadows[10] apartment last night about 11 p.m. when police say he beat and molested her." The reporter also noted both that "there's evidence that the father spanked the child in an effort to potty train the child on a regular basis" and that "It appears the child had been abused for a long time."

Two days later, an update on another station reported that the girl, who was now identified as 18 months old, had died, and the father had been charged with murder. The station juxtaposed videotape of the father in a prison uniform with a photograph of the child—clearly a baby—lying on her back on a couch, a pacifier in her mouth.

Similarly, when a 10-year-old girl in Gulfport, Mississippi, was murdered by a confessed serial killer, a photograph of the girl was shown along with videotape of her murderer in prison. In another story, photographs of a man accused of raping a 13-year-old girl, and then burying the newborn baby that was the result of that rape, were shown alongside the small, dug-up grave where the baby's body was found. A police mug shot of the man, who was the live-in boyfriend of the girl's mother, was also shown, with the caption containing the charges against him: "child molestation, statutory rape, concealing a death." He had not been charged with murder, the news noted, because it had yet to be determined whether the baby had died of natural causes prior to being buried.

In addition to the visual disparity between a seemingly helpless child or baby and a grown, powerful adult, the listing of charges beneath a photo helps to frame the suspect or assailant as guilty by identifying him with the crimes listed. Interviews that focused on the horrified or anguished reactions of neighbors or others also provided the audience with cues to the appropriate response to the crime while fulfilling television's imperative for emotionally gripping visuals.

For example, at a candlelight vigil for the murdered Gulfport girl, who was white, the camera provided close-ups of African American and white women wiping tears from their eyes and a spokeswoman choking up while addressing the crowd. The camera also closed in on the faces of both black and white children as they held flickering candles while a man's voice led them and the others in singing "Jesus loves the little children, loves the children of the world." In this way, the death of the girl is presented as a tragedy that transcends racial barriers and serves as a reminder that all children—regardless of race—are at risk.

Reporters also frequently told the viewers how they should feel about the victim and the crime. The story about the buried newborn was described as "bizarre and sad," and the actions of the accused as "horrible." The 10-year-old girl in Gulfport was a "tragic death" that "has made a heart-breaking change in the life of this Gulf Coast community." One reporter, referring to the "grisly claims" of the confessed killer, stated that if his confessions of murdering many others were true, his crimes "may be bigger and more shocking than any in history," so that it "almost seems that he's in competition of some type with Jeffrey Dahmer."[11]

Stories about the rape of elderly women also tended to depict the victims as innocent. These stories emphasized the heinous nature of the crime through the comments of reporters or interviewed sources and often identified the suspected rapist through photographs captioned with his name and the charges against him. Although pictures of the victim were not shown, the photo of the suspect—who generally appeared to be healthy and relatively young—created an image of imbalance in power and size when the victim was identified as being 70 or 80 years old.

Describing the injuries suffered also underscored the victim's vulnerability and frailty. For example, when a 31-year-old man was arrested and "charged with raping and sodomizing an 80-year-old woman" in her apartment, the suspect was identified in a photo with the caption "rape suspect." The reporter then announced that "the victim is in the hospital with cuts on her face and neck and a broken knee."

Unlike stories of rape of the elderly that emphasized the injuries to the women, the capture of a suspected serial rapist was more likely to focus on the rapist than on the injuries to his victims. As with the stories of murdered children, the reporter and those interviewed for the story emphasized the horror of the crime. In a story about a suspect "accused of terrorizing mostly elderly victims during a recent series of rapes," his criminal record and the fact that he was "released from prison just a year ago after serving only a third of his sentence for rape and manslaughter" were emphasized. His pattern of rape, according to the reporter, was to break into the women's homes and "savagely" attack his victims. A spokesperson with the county's pardons and paroles office then stated his department's "outrage that this fellow has evidently committed" these rapes, adding that, "If he did this, he's an animal, he's incorrigible."

Female victims also appeared innocent when they were killed as part of a shooting spree or group murder or when they were tortured or their bodies mutilated in a particularly gruesome manner by what appeared to be a psychopathic monster. Graphic details relating to the torture, along with visuals highlighting blood and gore, are key factors in placing the crime—and the criminal—beyond the pale of acceptable human behavior. For example, one story opened with videotape of police taking what appeared to be plastic trash bags from a building. The voice-over stated that "police are investigating the dismemberment of a woman. When the woman was reported missing, police searched her apartment and found her body cut into pieces." The scene then shifted to police carrying what was presumably part of a body out of the building on a stretcher. The voice-over intoned that "investigators think her killer used a circular saw." The visual gore and focus on dismemberment in this story were likely to be repugnant to most viewers—and this revulsion helps to establish the victim's innocence.

When nonelderly adult women were killed in murder sprees or as part of a larger group, they also appeared blameless. But this does not necessarily mean that the men who committed the crimes were blamed. Their guilt was at least partially absolved by their portrayal as mentally unbalanced and, therefore, not fully responsible for their actions. The picture of mental imbalance may be achieved through statements that underscore the murderer's instability and emphasize the unusual or bizarre circumstances of the murder.

In these scenarios, the women are peripheral to the story and their murders appear incidental, the result of their having the bad fortune (along with others similarly murdered or injured in the attack) to have been at the wrong place at the wrong time. For example, one news story about a man on a "carefully planned murder-suicide spree" opened with videotape of an ambulance and the reporter's voice-over: "A man suspected of shooting six people in North Georgia has been found tonight, dead, at the plant where he works." When the picture cut to the anchor's desk, the anchor stated, "After a manhunt that lasted all day, police tonight discovered the body of 23-year-old Jimmy Williams, Jr. They say he shot himself in the head. And that's our top story."

From the beginning, the story was framed by the murderer's own suicide—not by the shooting of his former girlfriend or others in the shooting spree. In fact, it wasn't until much later in the story that viewers learned that among Williams's victims was his former girl-friend and co-worker at the plant. This framing is likely the result of the news values or conventions of timeliness and immediacy, which emphasize that the most recent occurrence is most newsworthy. Nevertheless, the story emphasized the murderer's suicide and the finding of his body rather than the people whose lives he took or maimed. The story claimed that Williams snapped "in a fit of rage" and concluded with the reporter's noting both the lack of a clear motive and the possibility that the breakup with his former girlfriend or a misunderstanding about his job may have precipitated the killings:

> Police still have no clear motive on what was behind all this, what caused Jimmy Williams to snap in a fit of rage today. They say it is possible it may have been the breakup with his girlfriend and co-worker here at the plant or possibly the mistaken belief that he had been fired from his job. They say they may never know the answer.

The depiction of Williams as having "snap[ped] in a fit of rage" contradicts earlier parts of the report that emphasized that the murders were "carefully planned," that Williams previously had kid-napped another "girlfriend" and forced her to write out his murder plans and a will. According to the sheriff, Williams "went by the plan—step one, two, three—and in the end he did what he said he would do."

Clearly, the shootings were premeditated, carefully constructed and not the result of anyone's having spontaneously "snapped." The characterization of Williams as having snapped, however, explains his actions as the result of mental instability over which he presumably had no control. In this way, the news portrays Williams as not fully responsible for his actions.

Blaming the Victim

What if a woman is neither a child nor elderly, neither assaulted by someone characterized as mentally ill nor attacked as part of a group? Chances are she will be represented as somehow responsible for her own suffering because she was on drugs, drunk, not properly cautious, stupid, engaged in questionable activities, or involved in work or exhibiting behavior outside the traditional role of women. Her guilt is signified through statements—made by reporters, anchors, or interviewed sources—that seek to explain why the crime occurred within the context of her activities.

Sometimes, the concluding statement by the reporter or anchor casts doubt on the victim's innocence, which suggests that something she had done was ultimately responsible for the attack. For example, when a 35-year-old woman was shot in the head while driving in a car at 7 a.m., the anchor concluded the report by noting, "Police are investigating a possible drug connection and why the victim was so far from her home in Cumming so early in the morning." The underlying assumption was that if she had not been involved with drugs, if she were not where she did not belong at that early morning hour, she would still be alive.

Similarly, when a 24-year-old woman "slapped" a $9 million lawsuit against the Clayton County police department because, she claimed, a police officer raped her, the news report stated that the woman said the officer "arrested her for arguing with her husband." The report concluded with the anchor explaining why the officer had not been charged with rape: "Clayton police say they have a tough case on their hands. The woman has trouble remembering some of the details of what happened that night because she'd been drinking." If the woman hadn't been drunk, if she hadn't been arguing with her husband, she would not have been arrested and she would not be claiming rape. At best, she appears complicit in her own victimization; at worst, she is lying.

However, even when no drugs or alcohol are involved, when women are attacked in what is presumably the safety of their own homes or places of work, they still may be portrayed as guilty. For example, a woman who was shot when someone broke into her home while she was sleeping was described as "the head of discipline" at a nearby high school. The reporter added that "students say she is a strict disciplinarian." The story then cut to a student who stated: "She was really a hardball on getting on to students. It wasn't—I don't think she wanted enemies. It was just to get them in line, to get them straight."

Implied is that she was perhaps too strict—that she did, in fact, make enemies among the students she disciplined, and that a disgruntled student had shot her. If she had been less of a "hardball," and perhaps more traditionally nurturing and understanding, she might not have been harmed.

Another story began with the reporter's announcing that "a woman trying to do someone a favor has ended up a victim of rape." From the beginning, the rape is tied to her actions—that is, doing someone a favor. As the story unfolds, the audience is told that she let a man into the locked school building where she worked: "Police say the man got into the school by asking for a drink of water. The employee let him in, and he seized the opportunity." Here, it becomes clear that the employee is at fault, for she naively gave the rapist his opportunity to rape her.

Whether the doubt is cast at the end of the story or earlier, it is tied to an ideology that reflects cultural myths and patriarchal assumptions about the proper role and behavior of women. These myths and assumptions are embedded in the journalistic "why" of a story and ask why a woman was raped, beaten, or murdered—was it something she said or did? According to Mildred Pagelow (1981), "There is an interest in looking for the 'reasons' a woman was beaten that is similar to asking why a woman was raped, unlike in other crimes—for example, few people ask why a person was robbed" (p. 63).

Not all news accounts blamed or exonerated the victim, however. Shorter stories often did not provide enough information to assess guilt or innocence. These stories did not attempt to answer the "why" of the assault but reported information such as the discovery of a woman's body, that a man held his wife or girlfriend hostage, and that police are on the lookout for a rapist. The women in these stories were virtually invisible. Nevertheless, they represent the ever-present threats and dangers to women.

It should be emphasized that the presumed vulnerability associated with a female's extreme youth or old age is not always enough to guarantee immunity from charges of complicity in her victimization. She also must not have crossed the moral boundaries of socially appropriate female behavior. For example, a 10-year-old prostitute or an elderly drug dealer who is murdered or raped may be viewed as "asking for it."

Even when women are represented as innocent and their attackers are not deemed mentally unstable, though, the assailant is not necessarily represented as being at fault. When the victim is a child, it is often the mother who must bear the blame. For example, while the father of the 2-year-old girl was charged with physically and sexually assaulting her, an aunt and the child's mother—who, we are told, hadn't been around for a week—were charged with cruelty to children. In the story about the teenager raped by her mother's live-in boyfriend, who later buried her newborn baby, the girl's mother was arrested along with the boyfriend. And when the serial murderer was arrested for the kidnapping and murder of the 10-year-old girl in Gulfport, Mississippi, her mother also was arrested, the reporter stated, "to ensure that she will testify."

In these reports, the victim is blameless. But the mother, we are told, must bear some—if not all—of the responsibility, for she was presumably in a position to halt the violence, to protect her child, but did not. Thus, the news delineates the appropriate role and obligations of motherhood, as well as the dangers of ignoring those responsibilities.

Gender, Race, and Class

This study found that all women who are the victims of violence—regardless of race or class—are represented within the news as potentially to blame for causing their own victimization. The burden of guilt lies with the victim, and only when cultural norms and values concerning children, the elderly, torture, and mass murderers conflict with accepted myths and assumptions about women and violence can female victims be considered innocent.

This does not mean that race and class are irrelevant to the portrayal of women in the news. As the quantitative part of this study indicated, crimes against white women with money are more likely to be considered newsworthy than crimes against black women without money. But race and class also are inseparable from the representation of gender.

Barry Brummett (1991) points out that TV news personalizes complex and abstract issues, reducing them to easily grasped images with which the audience can identify. Identification therefore depends on the "individual's own situation, opinions, actions, choices and decisions" (Brummett, 1991, p. 172). Where gender, race, and class are concerned, understanding may be hampered by ideology, which works to reinforce stereotypes about African Americans, women, poverty, and violence.

Even the lack of racial identification can be a cause of speculation and stereotyping among viewers if some aspect of the stereotype is present. For example, there was no photo or other racial identification of the woman who was shot in the head while driving in a neighborhood far from home at 7 a.m. However, some viewers might well have concluded that she was African American based on the implication that drugs were involved.

The murdered baby, beaten and sexually assaulted by her father, would have appeared innocent whether she was black or white. However, she was identified in the photo as black, her father similarly was identified as African American in the story's footage, and they were living in East Lake Meadows, a subsidized public housing project, at the time she was murdered. Thus, in making sense of this story, some viewers may have drawn on the myth of the black man as rapist and other stereotypes about black men, violence, sex, and poverty to conclude that black men are bad fathers who are prone to violence and sexual assault. The man accused of raping the 13-year-old girl and then burying her baby also was identified as black through the use of a photograph that showed him with his girlfriend—the raped girl's mother—who was white. This not only perpetuates the rape myth but is linked to cultural stereotypes about black men defiling white women—in this case, both the daughter and the mother.

Similarly, news reports that the mother of the murdered African American baby had been gone for a week and was charged with cruelty to children reinforces racist and sexist beliefs about black women as negligent and inadequate mothers. The white mother of the 13-year-old rape victim, on the other hand, also may be seen as negligent and inadequate. However, this portrayal is individualistic, tied to the specific circumstances of her daughter's rape by the mother's boyfriend. She does not, after all, represent the failings of all white mothers.

Summary

In an attempt to explain the "why" of violence against women, news reports tend to blame either the victim or the assailant. *Who* gets faulted is a function of an underlying ideology of male supremacy that separates women into virgin-whore or good girl-bad girl categories based on cultural stereotypes, myths, and assumptions concerning the proper role of women. Children and elderly women are generally considered innocent victims because they are presumed to be weak and vulnerable. Acts of violence that are considered particularly gruesome serve to absolve the victim of blame, for it is difficult to argue that anyone—no matter what she has done—deserves to be tortured or mutilated.

But when the victim is not considered helpless because of her age, she frequently is represented as in some way responsible for the assault. She was where she shouldn't have been, she took a stupid risk, she did not ensure her own safety. Women, unless they are young and weak or old and infirm,[12] are responsible for their own protection, the news tells us—even as it denies their ability to take care of themselves. And if they do not protect themselves, they are at fault.

In addition, the representation of women as victims of violence cannot be divorced from the discourses of race and class. The victimization of wealthy, white women appears deserving of coverage; the victimization of poor, black women does not. Within this framework, racial and male supremacist ideologies converge to establish blame for black female victims beyond what is generally assigned to white women.

By presenting stories of violence against women as separate, discrete incidents, the news also reinforces the idea that this violence is a matter of isolated pathology or deviance, related only to the particular circumstances of those involved and unconnected to the larger structure of patriarchal domination and control. This mirage of individual pathology denies the social roots of violence against women and relieves the larger society of any obligation to end it.

As Keith Soothill and Sylvia Walby (1991) found in their study of newspaper coverage of sex crime, the media "are very loath to consider that sex crime may be related to men's and women's position in society" (p. 36), preferring instead to focus on the few individuals who commit particularly gruesome or heinous atrocities. This assessment of the news media's reluctance to relate sex crimes to the social order appears true for nonsexual crimes against women as well.

Reporters and editors believe that to do so would be to bias the news and that advocates for battered and raped women are unreliable news sources because they are not neutral (see Chapter 6). Furthermore, they claim that they are simply presenting information the public has a right to—and wants to—know. They have argued that they should not be in the position of censoring public information provided by the police (Benedict, 1992). However, the withholding of public information is not without precedent. Journalists routinely withhold public information, such as a raped woman's name and address, to protect her, and they also do not disclose the identity of juveniles who are either criminal assailants or victims. As victims and advocates for rape survivors and battered women make clear, many of the details of sexual assault or other acts of violence serve to revictimize the victim, just as surely as would public identification.

There are, of course, times when the release of details—such as the location in which an attack occurred—is useful in alerting women to potential danger. However, details involving the victims' actions prior to, during, or after the assault are not necessary to warn others of a rapist in the neighborhood—or of the dangers of allowing strange men into their homes or places of employment. In the story about the school employee who allowed a man into the school building and then was raped by him, for example, the man had been apprehended and was in police custody at the time the story was aired. Hence, information about how the man gained access to the building served no social function in terms of warning women about a rapist on the loose. Had he remained at large, though, it would have been sufficient for the reporter or anchor simply to have noted that police are urging women to make sure their doors are locked. Similarly, the audience does not need to know that police suspect drugs were involved in the murder of a woman shot in her car. Such information serves to stigmatize the victim when she may not, in fact, be a drug abuser. The allusion to a drug connection also reinforces the good girl-bad girl dichotomy, supporting the erroneous assumption that good girls—that is, women who do not abuse drugs or otherwise transgress the moral and social boundaries of appropriate female behavior—are safe. In reality, no woman is safe from the threat of male violence, just as no woman deserves to be blamed for having been battered, raped, or otherwise abused.

The reporting of information that represents the victim as guilty, as somehow at fault for contributing to, causing, or not protecting herself from violence, is often painful and embarrassing to the victim—if she is still alive—and her family. It is not uncommon, for example, for rape survivors to blame themselves for having been raped (Gordon & Riger, 1989, p. 44). This internalization of blame, reinforced by the media, makes it more difficult for the victim to heal emotionally.

Nevertheless, many journalists and others argue that details that could be interpreted as blaming the victim, such as that she opened the door to a rapist or might be involved with drugs, are a legitimate part of the story. This argument is, however, a red herring, for it posits standard news conventions and practices as the only legitimate way to gather and present the news. The point is that the legitimate, conventional ways of presenting the news are often harmful to women who have been victimized. That harm occurs on both a personal and societal level, for although news coverage that blames the victim may be a source of humiliation, guilt, or anguish to the women, it also reinforces the very myths and stereotypes that the many victims have internalized and that society uses to keep women in their place. The claim of legitimacy should not divert attention from the effects of "legitimate" coverage. What's needed is a new definition of legitimacy for news coverage of violence against women—one that respects rather than blames the victim.

Notes

1. The late evening newscast was chosen for uniformity because although the early evening broadcasts all began at 6 p.m., one lasted for half an hour, and the other two were an hour long.

2. WAGA's network affiliation has since shifted from CBS to Fox.

3. Although the goal was to tape newscasts for 8 weeks, technical difficulties cut a few days from the beginning point of the study. This delay was not considered crucial to the outcome.

4. A hierarchy of violence was established for consistency in coding cases of multiple types of violence, such as when a woman is raped and murdered. In this case, murder would be the primary type of violence and rape would be secondary.

5. The intercoder agreement for the class status of both the assailant and victim was 80%, which reflects the difficulty of defining class. For this study, class was coded as either poor, working class, middle class/professional, upper-middle class/wealthy, or unknown. Coding was based on both occupation and residence, as well as on the explicit identification by the reporter or anchor. If the victim was identified as living in "public housing," or a related term for subsidized housing, she was coded as poor. However, her class would have been coded as unknown if the news noted the name of the housing complex without mentioning that it was subsidized housing, because

most viewers are not necessarily familiar with the names of all but the most infamous housing projects in the metropolitan Atlanta area. (The infamous ones would have resulted in a coding of poor.) If the victim lived in Buckhead, well-known as a wealthy neighborhood in Atlanta, but no further information was provided, her class status was coded as unknown because it could not be assumed that all Buckhead residents are wealthy. In the case of a battered woman who was routinely identified in the media as a "millionaire," the category coded was upper-middle class/wealthy.

6. Permission to quote from one of the station's newscasts was conditional on stories produced by that station not being identified as such. Hence, none of the stories are identified by the stations that produced and aired them.

7. Intercoder reliability for individual categories was as follows:

primary type of violence, 85%; race of assailant, 95%; race of victim, 95%; sex of assailant, 100%; number of victims, 95%; number of assailants, 100%; age of primary victim, 85%; class of victim, 80%; class of assailant, 80%; context of coverage, 90%.

8. Television news generally does not show photos of rape victims unless they also have been murdered.

9. Twenty stories, representing 10% of the total number of stories coded, were originally randomly selected for further analysis. The remaining 12 stories were chosen to augment that sample based on their proximity to the previously examined stories on the videotapes. This method of choosing stories is considered appropriate for this analysis given that the goal is to underscore and highlight the workings of ideology rather than to achieve statistical representativeness.

10. East Lake Meadows is a public housing project in Atlanta, and its identification within the news story signifies the victim and her father as poor. The quantitative part of this study coded their class position as "unknown" because East Lake Meadows was not identified within the story as a public housing project. Hence, readers, as well as coders, may not have recognized the name and could have assumed it was a private apartment complex. Discursive analysis, however, requires familiarity with nuance and details that is often unnecessary in quantitative studies.

11. Dahmer was convicted of murdering, dismembering, and cannibalizing his victims.

12. Women who are physically disabled also may be represented as innocent because, like children and elderly women, they are presumed to be—and often are—frail and vulnerable.

C H A P T E R

5

News of Self-Defense

$\mathbf{F}$ear of rape, battering, or other violence at the hands of a man or men has circumscribed the lives of most women (Bannister, 1991; Bograd, 1988; Gardner, 1990; Gordon & Riger, 1989; Stanko, 1985). Frequently, it determines what a woman will wear, where she can go, her mode of transportation, and her hour of departure or return (Koss, 1993). Women's magazines often run articles detailing precautions that should be taken, and most college campuses and communities offer self-defense classes for women. As Pauline Bart and Eileen Moran (1993) state, women's lives "are at best constrained and at worst seriously damaged by violence and fear of violence" (p. xiii).

The discursive analysis presented here examines how women who have succeeded in defending themselves against male violence are portrayed within the news. It asks whether the mythology and cultural expectations concerning women who fight back differ from those involving women who appear to be passive victims. Indeed, women who engage in self-defense can be seen as violating gender role expectations in the simple act of refusing to be passive:

All feminist rape analysts agree that traditional female socialization sets up a women to be raped rather than to avoid rape when attacked. Deference to male authority is presented as the only appropriate behavior if a woman is to acquire a husband. (Bart & O'Brien, 1985, p. 105)

This chapter presents a discursive analysis of two local television news stories about women who defended themselves against male violence. In one story, a battered woman was on trial for killing her husband; in the other, a woman successfully fought off an attempted rape.

The analysis indicates that the representation of women who fight back is tied to whether their actions are considered justified. Justification, however, is not determined by the type or degree of abuse a woman is defending herself against but by whether she can be seen as having contributed to or provoked the violence against her. As with women who are the victims of violence but are not reported to have fought back, the depiction of women who defend themselves is steeped in cultural myths and stereotypes concerning appropriate behavior for women.

The stories examined were broadcast in Atlanta, Georgia, during the 11 p.m. news. They were chosen because they involved the two most extensively covered stories concerning women who fought back against rape and battering during a period of data collection spanning June 30 through August 31, 1991.

This is not to suggest there were a significant number of other stories about women defending themselves against male aggression. Stories of women who fight back are relatively rare within the news, despite the fact that three of four female victims of violence either physically or verbally resist their attackers (U.S. Department of Justice, 1994b). Indeed, of 32 television news stories about anti-woman violence that were selected for the study in Chapter 4, only one other local story, in addition to the two examined here, included a woman defending herself. That other story actually had two plot lines: The rape of a woman was the primary focus of the story, but it included interviews and videotape concerning another woman who had chased the same rapist away from her home with a shovel before he could attack her.

Notably, all three of these stories of self-defense involved white women, despite the fact that Atlanta's population is approximately two-thirds African American and the larger metropolitan area is about one-fourth African American. African American women appear to be underrepresented in news stories of women who fight back against male violence, as well as in other news stories of violence against women.[1]

Of the two stories examined here, one story involved an unnamed woman who fought back against a man believed to be a serial rapist.[2] The attacks had occurred in the wealthy, white, Atlanta neighborhood of Buckhead. Previous news reports had indicated that the man, dubbed the "Buckhead rapist" by the media, had raped four women, mostly in open areas and parking garages. His modus operandi was to jump his victims from behind and beat, as well as rape, them. The rapist, who sometimes robbed his victims, often prevented the women from seeing his face and threatened to kill them if they looked at him.

In the other story to be analyzed, a jury rendered a misdemeanor verdict—involuntary manslaughter—in the murder trial of Katrine Bursheim, a battered woman who shot her abusive husband, John Bursheim, in self-defense when he attacked her with a knife. News reports emphasized that she was a 75-year-old millionaire married for the fifth time to a much younger man. Testimony during the course of the trial also indicated that she had admitted on her wedding day that she had "bought" her younger husband. Testimony indicated that John, who was 58 years old at the time of the shooting, had abused her physically and emotionally: He had pulled her arm out of joint, cut up her credit cards, and forced her to sign blank checks. After Katrine survived a bout with lung cancer, which her husband expected her to die from, he removed her belongings to a back bedroom of the house and locked her in the room, refusing to let her leave, make phone calls, or hire a nurse to take care of her. He secretly recorded her conversations, bilked her out of most of her million-dollar estate, and threatened to put her in a nursing home.

Katrine Bursheim testified that she and her husband were arguing about finances when he attacked her with a kitchen knife. The knife cut her thumb, but she managed to knock it out of his hand. When he leaned over to pick it up, she reached across a nearby table and grabbed a gun, which she had given him for Valentine's Day five days earlier, and shot him.

The Bursheim story was broadcast July 5, 1991, on WAGA, which at the time was the Atlanta CBS affiliate. The Buckhead rapist story aired August 13, 1991, on WXIA, an NBC affiliate. Both stories opened the evening's newscast.

The Battered-Woman Defense

The story announcing the verdict in the Katrine Bursheim murder trial indicates from the very beginning that Bursheim quite literally got away with murder. It opens with the male voice of the jury foreman announcing, "We, the jury, find the defendant guilty of misdemeanor, involuntary manslaughter." The camera shows the silver-haired Katrine Bursheim seated in court. The voice of the male anchor then cuts in: "Showing little emotion, a 75-year-old Cobb County woman is convicted of shooting her husband in the back."

By emphasizing in his first sentence that Bursheim shot her husband in the back, the anchor implies that Bursheim may not have been in danger at the time of the shooting, that her husband may, in fact, have been walking away from her. There is no mention of the knife John wielded or that he was bending over to pick it up when Katrine shot him.

The characterization of a defendant's emotional state when the verdict is read is a standard feature of news reporting. The choice of words is determined by the reporter's assessment, which is, of course, informed by her or his own biases and codes of interpretation. Thus, if a defendant appears unmoved by the verdict, if the defendant's face and demeanor appear unchanged, the reporter might describe the emotional state as impassive, numb, or, in the case of Katrine Bursheim, as "showing little emotion." The characterization of Katrine as lacking emotion suggests she was unfeeling, which could further imply that she was without remorse or guilt for what she has done. Thus, from that first sentence, Katrine Bursheim could be seen as a cold, calculating killer, someone who murders not in self-defense, for her husband's back was turned, but for some other, unnamed reason.

The anchor's next four sentences hint that the verdict was too lenient:

The jury could have found Katrine Bursheim guilty of murder. But jurors accepted her argument that she was an abused wife who shot and killed in self-defense. The crime they found her guilty of is only a misdemeanor. It could mean she never spends a day in prison.

The lightness of the verdict is underscored by emphasizing (a) the possibility of a murder verdict versus the jury's actual misdemeanor verdict, (b) that the jury "only" found her guilty of a misdemeanor, and (c) that she might never spend "a day in prison."

After the anchor's introduction, the scene moves to the courthouse, where the voice of a male reporter is heard over videotape of the courtroom:

Katrine Bursheim never denied she killed her fifth husband, John. But she claims self-defense—the battered wife defense—after years of what witnesses saw as physical and mental abuse. Prosecutors claim the 75-year-old millionaire planned the killing when she realized her husband had made off with most of her fortune. [The camera cuts to a teenage male on the stand.] A neighborhood teenager testified she asked him to move the body from the house 14 hours after John Bursheim was shot.

The reporter's presence at the courthouse lends credibility to his report, for he is, after all, in a position to provide an eyewitness account and assessment of the jury's verdict—and Bursheim's actions. In addition, the coverage seems to raise more questions than it answers. The lack of definitive answers tends to work against Bursheim, providing a discursive opening that invites speculation about her motives and veracity. For example, emphasizing the number of times she was married raises questions about her character and about what happened to her previous four husbands: Did she kill them, too? Were her former husbands the source of her wealth?[3]

In noting that her most recent husband "had made off with most of her fortune," the reporter presents a motive for his murder. Bursheim's claim of self-defense is bolstered by the reporter's stating that witnesses testified to years of what they saw as physical and mental abuse. But the "abuse" is never defined and remains vague. The ambiguity of the term raises still more questions: Is a slap on the hand considered physical abuse? Is yelling a form of mental abuse? Certainly, such abuse would not justify homicide. The omission of any explanation of the abuse—including Katrine Bursheim's claim

that her husband attacked her with a knife when she shot him—
weakens the self-defense argument and disconnects his murder from
his abusive behavior.

That Katrine Bursheim did not call police or an ambulance after
shooting her husband but waited 14 hours and then sought to have
his body removed from the house reinforces the anchor's characterization of Bursheim as being without feeling or emotion. She did not,
after all, call an ambulance or a doctor—or the police. This depiction,
however, is contradicted by Bursheim herself when she appears
before the camera outside the courthouse. She is clearly distraught,
and she begins to cry as she talks to reporters:

> If I had known then what I know now about him, I would never have
> married him. But I was blindly in love with him at the beginning, and
> it just slowly eroded with his abuse and neglect. [Bursheim's face
> contorts, her voice cracks and she sobs.] But I guess somewhere in the
> bottom of my heart I'll always remember him the way I thought he was
> when I married him.

Far from seeming cold and calculating, Katrine Bursheim appears
to have genuinely loved—and may still love—John Bursheim. She
concedes that she was duped, that her marriage was a mistake based
on an illusion, the result of being "blindly in love." She acknowledges
that her husband turned out to be different from "the way I thought
he was." She admits, in essence, that she was gullible and "would
never have married him" if she had known what he was really like.
There is a pathetic quality about Bursheim's sobbing for the man
whose love she once believed in, for it now appears to have been
based on his greed and her gullibility.

When gullibility is associated with the young, it is considered
innocence and naïveté. However, given Bursheim's age, it signifies
her as a foolish, old woman who should have known better. She
appears to be to blame not only for marrying someone much
younger—which, although acceptable for men, is still considered
scandalous for women—but for not recognizing that he was interested only in her for her wealth. Had she not been so foolish, so
"blindly in love," she would not have been in a situation in which
she was abused. The abuse, then, appears to be at least partially her
fault.

Bursheim appears to undermine her defense when she talks about her love eroding "with his abuse and neglect." Not only does the "abuse" remain undefined, but it is linked to the more benign "neglect," with its connotation of simply being ignored. Thus, Katrine Bursheim appears to be a foolish old woman who married unwisely but was not seriously abused.

It is clear from the news report that John Bursheim took Katrine's money. What is less clear in this story is whether he also may have been an adulterer. After Katrine's statement to the media, the audience is shown a photograph of a middle-aged John Bursheim with an unidentified, attractive, young, blonde woman by his side. The reporter's voice-over states, "The misdemeanor verdict means Mrs. Bursheim will have a better chance of reclaiming her money—more than a million is tied up in her dead husband's estate." The camera then cuts to Katrine Bursheim's defense attorney, who states, "Even her jewelry, even her mother's wedding ring, is in *his* estate."

The photo of John Bursheim with a young, attractive woman suggests that he may have had other women in his life, an implication that could have been reinforced by informing the audience that John Bursheim rarely lived with his wife and did, as Katrine's attorney noted in other news reports, run around with other women. This information, however, was not included here. The fact that Katrine Bursheim's money, jewelry—even her mother's wedding ring—are in his estate supports the characterization of John Bursheim as an opportunist who married Katrine for her wealth.

That John Bursheim made off with Katrine's money and may have been sexually involved with other women provides a motive for his murder. Indeed, the reporter, and an interviewed juror, remain unconvinced that Katrine Bursheim was as abused as she claimed or that she really needed to kill her husband to defend herself. The reporter noted that although jurors agreed that Bursheim acted in self-defense, they also believed "she used excessive force" and that her husband wasn't "as horrible as the defense wanted them to believe." A white male juror was then interviewed saying, "We didn't feel like she was as abused as she was made out to be. . . . It didn't play in the long run, really."

The question of how abused Katrine was and the suggestion that she used "excessive force" are key elements framing Katrine's guilt.

They also are intertwined, for the juror and reporter imply that her actions were excessive given that the abuse was not that serious. The standard to which Katrine Bursheim is being held is, as Gillespie (1989) notes, a male standard that assumes that both combatants are male and of equal physical strength and ability. The "deadly force doctrine" stipulates that deadly force is justified as self-defense only when it is necessary as a way for the woman to protect herself from imminent death or serious bodily injury (Ewing, 1987; Gillespie, 1989).

The belief that Katrine used excessive force ignores the fact that the 75-year-old woman was defending herself against a man considerably stronger and younger than she. Clearly, hand-to-hand combat would have provided no protection. Nor would attempting to grab the knife from her husband and using it against him. In all probability, the gun provided her best chance for self-defense. And although she presumably could have shot him in the arm or leg, it is understandable that the panicked and injured elderly woman would shoot him in the back as he bent down to retrieve the knife she had managed to knock out of his hand. By presenting the juror's opinion without balancing it with the defense's argument and justification for the shooting, the news implies both that Bursheim was not seriously abused and that she used excessive force in defending herself.

The reporter finished his report by noting the date for sentencing and that Bursheim "could wind up with only probation," clearly implying that probation is a very light sentence for her crime. Back in the studio, the anchor then concluded the story by stating, "Bursheim is free on bond tonight. She said she's looking forward to returning to her job as executive secretary at the Chattahoochee Country Club." Bursheim appears to have received no more than a slap on the wrist. She is, after all, returning to her country club.

This story denied the terror and abuse under which Bursheim said she lived and that was the basis of her defense. In effect, it denied that she was a battered woman. The news also made her complicit in her own victimization by implying she should have known better than to marry a fortune hunter. In the end, the story suggests that she successfully avoided having to pay the just price for "shooting her husband in the back."

The Buckhead Rapist Attack

The story of the woman who defended herself against a man who attacked her began with the female co-anchor's announcing, "He could be the Buckhead rapist. He's still alive tonight—thanks to quick medical treatment."

The male co-anchor then provided more details:

> But a very strange twist tonight. The blood transfusion that saved this man's life is slowing down the investigation. Here is the situation so far. The man is accused of attacking a woman last night in Buckhead. She had a knife and stabbed him in the neck. [The camera cuts to the crime scene, where there are police, as well as a considerable amount of blood, on the porch of a home.] He's still in critical condition tonight at Piedmont Hospital. The man lost a lot of blood before he got help, so much so, in fact, that he was given several transfusions of blood from other people. [A graphic appears in the background of the crime scene with the title "Buckhead assault" and a three-point outline of the situation: "(1) still in critical condition; (2) received several blood transfusions; (3) police can't match blood sample with rapist."] So tonight police tell us they can't take a blood sample that is to make a case against him as the Buckhead rapist. Again, because he has too much other blood in his system. [The camera cuts to the blood-splattered wall of the porch and the sidewalk.] Neal Craig has the latest on this investigation and some women who say this guy got what he deserved.

This introduction establishes the primary details of the story as well as the guilt of the attacker, for there is never any question that he attacked the woman who stabbed him on what appears to be the porch of her home.[4]

The camera's focus on the amount of blood lost by the attacker—on the wall and floor of the porch as well as on the sidewalk—coupled with the description of the transfusions necessary to save his life, attests to the seriousness of his injury. The fact that police suspect he may be the Buckhead rapist establishes him as a dangerous person. The anchor's final statement introducing the reporter also suggests that "this guy got what he deserved." As the rest of the story makes clear, there appears to be no doubt that he deserved it.

After the anchor's introduction, the camera cuts to what is presumably a Buckhead neighborhood. A woman in T-shirt and shorts is jogging; a man is jogging with his dog. Both are white and appear young and healthy. The reporter's voice is heard over this street scene:

People in the neighborhood where the attack happened are more aware now they need to watch out for each other. Everyone I talked to says they'll try harder not to put themselves in potential harm. But if confronted with danger, they'll strike back, too.

A white couple is then shown walking down the street, and the camera cuts to a head shot of the woman, identified only as Christie. The interview follows:

Reporter: You agreed with what she did?
Christie: Yes.
Reporter: And you'd do the same thing?
Christie: I think it would be hard for me to harm someone else in that way, but I think I probably would have done the same thing.

The shot expands, and Christie is shown standing next to her male companion. The camera cuts to another white woman who is said to have agreed with the actions of the woman who defended herself. She states, "Because if she hadn't fought back, she may be the one laying in the hospital or dead already. She was incredibly brave to fight back, which a lot of women won't—and they need to, I think."

The statements of those interviewed not only support the actions of the woman who fought back, commending her as "incredibly brave," but also establish her actions as a model that other women would do well to emulate, even if they think "it would be hard . . . to harm someone else in that way." Fighting back—even if it means killing the attacker—is legitimized as the only way to avoid being raped or murdered.

After validating the appropriateness of the woman's act of self-defense, the concluding portion of the story argues that the attacker got what he deserved. The audience is shown a document that establishes the deviant background of the attacker by listing his criminal record. The reporter states,

The man knifed in the incident has a police record dating back to 1986—most offenses for car theft. Two people in the neighborhood where the attack happened now tell me their cars were broken into last night—but they didn't notice because of all the other excitement.

The implication is that the car break-ins were the work of the attacker, who now appears to be a petty thief and vandal as well as a serial rapist.

Analysis

There are significant differences in the representations of Katrine Bursheim and the unidentified woman who defended herself against an attacker in Buckhead. However, these differences do not appear to be related to the fact that one man was killed and the other wasn't. For had the man presumed to be the Buckhead rapist died of his wounds, it is unlikely that the woman who stabbed him would have been accused of excessive force. The stabbing, we are told, would clearly have killed him were it not for quick medical intervention in the form of blood transfusions.

However, other factors may have contributed to the differences in the representations of the two stories. Katrine Bursheim apparently made no attempt to try to save her husband's life once she shot him. Instead, she waited 14 hours before trying to have the body removed. Presumably, the woman who stabbed the alleged Buckhead rapist acted more quickly to get medical assistance for her attacker.

But what Bursheim and the Buckhead woman did after defending themselves in all probability does not play as large a role in their portrayals as do cultural myths and assumptions concerning women and violence. The two stories of women fighting back indicate that the act of self-defense appears justified only when the women's actions occur within the framework of patriarchal notions of appropriate gender roles and behavior. Women who step outside that boundary may be represented as unjustified in fighting back; those who remain within that socially sanctioned circle appear justified in their actions.

In Bursheim's case, stereotypes about age also converged with those concerning women and violence to deny that she was, indeed, a battered woman acting in self-defense. Bursheim was represented as literally having gotten away with murder, as complicit in her own victimization because she married a man much younger than herself. Given that women her age are supposed to be "old enough to know better," Katrine Bursheim appears to be the stereotypical "foolish old woman." This characterization makes her complicit in her own victimization at the hands of her husband, for she not only made the mistake of marrying him, but she did not recognize him for the opportunist he apparently was. And if she is complicit in her victimization, then John Bursheim cannot be fully responsible for the abuse. Although he may have been a scoundrel and a thief, the news implies, he did not deserve to die for those offenses. Of course, most people would rightly agree, at least in this culture, that being a scoundrel and a thief should not be punishable by death. However, the implication of this characterization of John Bursheim is that it obscures—even denies—that he could also have been a batterer and an attempted murderer.

In addition, omitting the details of her abuse, including that John Bursheim was wielding a knife at the time Katrine Bursheim shot him, makes the abuse appear insignificant—certainly not life threatening or of the degree that would warrant his death. The news also emphasized that John Bursheim was shot in the back, which casts doubt on Katrine's claim of self-defense. Statements from the anchor, reporter, and a member of the jury were skeptical of the severity of the abuse and declared Katrine's action excessive. This denies not only that Katrine was a battered woman but that the shooting was justifiable as an act of self-defense.

The stabbing of the man presumed to be the Buckhead rapist, on the other hand, was represented as a courageous act of self-defense, entirely justifiable given the attacker's actions and his criminal background. That he had attacked the unidentified woman and deserved to be critically injured or even killed is never in doubt. She is a heroine, a model for other women in similar circumstances.

The Buckhead woman's actions contradict the conventional wisdom concerning the appropriate response to an attack by a potential rapist, which is that the woman should remain passive because an aggressive defense is likely to agitate the assailant further and result in more serious injury and that using guile and attempting to talk the rapist out of committing the crime are effective. Research by Pauline Bart and Patricia O'Brien (1985), however, indicates that women who fight back—as did the Buckhead woman—are more likely to *avoid* rape. Bart and O'Brien found that trying to talk a rapist out of committing the crime is relatively useless and that pleading with the rapist is associated with *being* raped. Their findings not only challenge the advice traditionally given to women but indicate that the "avoidance myths" serve as "mechanisms of social control, keeping women down and dependent" (p. 113). To encourage women to fight back, Bart and O'Brien concluded, not only would help women avoid being raped but would also challenge the status quo by encouraging women to break with traditional role expectations:

> The myths about rape and rape avoidance would have us believe that women will not be raped if we restrict our behavior sufficiently, if we are unwilling, if we reason, nurture or use guile. Thus it is no wonder that until recently women jurors were considered unsympathetic to rape victims. All the information they have been given implied that they and women like them, "good" women, could not be raped. If a woman were raped, either she wanted it, or she deserved it, or she was stupid and naive; and in the case of rape, stupidity and naivete apparently are crimes justifying rape. (p. 114)

The difference in representation within the Buckhead rapist story and that of Katrine Bursheim is attributable to several factors, not the least of which is that the Buckhead woman apparently did not violate any of the social or moral boundaries considered appropriate for women. The two stories represent opposite sides of the same coin—that coin being patriarchal assumptions about the proper role of women. The Buckhead woman was, presumably, about to enter her home when she was attacked on her porch by a stranger. Unlike Katrine Bursheim, she did not make the mistake of inviting him into her home prior to his attack. She apparently had done nothing "wrong"—which is to say, outside the socially defined role for women—to warrant the attack and was therefore innocent of provocation or complicity.

In addition, Katrine Bursheim was married to the man she was defending herself against; the woman in Buckhead presumably had no prior relationship with her attacker. In a society in which marital rape has only relatively recently been recognized as a crime in many states and in which battering has for too long been viewed as a male privilege within marriage, one might well ask whether Bursheim's marital status worked against her in her representation within the news.

It is worth noting, too, that the perspective presented in the Bursheim story was primarily that of the anchor, reporter, and jurist, all of whom were male. Conversely, the story about the woman who defended herself in Buckhead was framed by female sources who lauded the woman's courage and told the reporter that the assailant "got what he deserved." The difference in perspective between the two stories may be tied to the gender of those framing the story. This is speculative and does not deny the importance of patriarchal myths and assumptions in shaping the news, the impact of organizational policies and considerations, or the subjectivity of individual report-ers.[5] Nevertheless, research indicates that women speak differently and have values that differ from those of men because their lives have been engendered differently (Gilligan, 1982; Kramarae, 1981). So it is not unreasonable to assume that women—most of whom have been taught from an early age to fear male violence—would understand violence and self-defense differently than would men.

It also should not be surprising that both Katrine Bursheim and the Buckhead woman are represented as affluent, white women. Bursheim was often described as a millionaire, and the theft of her money by her husband was used by the prosecution to provide a motive for his murder; the Buckhead woman was presumed to be white and upper-middle class, based on the neighborhood shown in the news as well as the large, tiled porch in front of her house. It also is well-known in Atlanta that Buckhead housing is the most expen-sive in the city. Thus, the woman who attacked the alleged Buckhead rapist in self-defense, in light of no contradictory information, is presumed to be both white and well-to-do.

The fact that no African American women were represented as defending themselves in the 32 stories examined is indicative of a bias in news coverage that considers white women more newswor-thy, particularly if they are wealthy. However, statistics indicate that African American women may be more likely to defend themselves against male violence than white women. The wife-to-husband ratio for murder among spouses differs significantly among blacks and whites, with black women the victims of spousal murder 59% of the time, compared with white women, who are the victims of spousal murder 74% of the time (U.S. Department of Justice, 1994c).

Gender, class, race, and age are inseparable in the representation of women and self-defense, as is the case with all violence against women. Relations of domination and control occur within the context of the interlocking nature of multiple oppressions, with the news perpetuating racist and classist stereotypes and assumptions at the same time that it reflects and maintains patriarchal notions of the proper role of women in society. The result is that, within the news, it doesn't matter whether a woman is successful in defending herself against violence. Whether or not she fights back and wins, she is still viewed through an ideological prism bound by social notions of race, class, and acceptable behavior for women.

Notes

1. This could be partially attributable to the possibility that African American women are less likely than white women to report abuse to the police.

2. Subsequent DNA tests showed that the man was not the same person who had raped the four women in Buckhead. The real Buckhead rapist—who had not, in fact, limited his activities to the Buckhead area—was convicted almost a year later.

3. In fact, Katrine had inherited more than a million dollars from her previous husband, a Florida land developer who had died of Alzheimer's disease.

4. The specific location of the stabbing and whether the house was the woman's home or somebody else's were never clarified in the story.

5. Although studies indicate that women and men have different ways of viewing and responding to the world (see, for example, Gilligan, 1982), research into the effects of gender on news content is inclusive. In summarizing much of the literature on the subject, van Zoonen (1994) concluded that the organizational workings of mass cultural production do "not leave much room for individual autonomy" (p. 64) so that "to expect that an increase in women communicators will influence media content in a desired feminist direction, is theoretically and strategically unsound" (p. 65). However, a number of other researchers (see, for example, Byerly, in press; Meyers, 1992; Rapping, 1994) have found that feminism and individual women within news and television production have made a gender-related difference in media content.

"Unusualness" and Crime News

Crime reporters daily face the question of what to cover among the vast offerings of rapes, batterings, murders, and other crimes that occur. Ultimately, those stories they consider most newsworthy appear in the pages of newspapers or are broadcast over the air.

But how do reporters make those determinations? What standards do they apply in deciding which stories are deserving of public attention? More specifically, how do they negotiate the social constructs of gender, race, and class in the determination of newsworthiness concerning violence against women?

This study attempts to answer these questions. It seeks to understand how reporters understand, rationalize, and make decisions concerning newsworthiness as it relates to violent crimes against women. In doing this, it examines the process by which journalists, as members of an interpretive community (Zelizer, 1992, 1993), create meaning through a collective understanding of professional practices, norms, and newsworthiness.

The findings indicate that the journalistic conception of unusualness, together with the lack of a concrete definition of news, protects reporters from charges of gender, race, and class bias while at the same time obscuring coverage that is, in fact, biased against women, people of color, the poor, and the working class.[1] The study also concludes that reporter reliance on police spokespersons as "legitimate" sources ensures that the police perspective is the predominant viewpoint presented.

In-depth interviews were conducted with nine local journalists in the Atlanta metropolitan area. Most of the eight reporters and one editor interviewed were involved in covering the killing of Sara Tokars.[2] The murder was used by reporters in the interviews as both an example and a focal point for discussion.[3]

Sara Tokars's death, which occurred November 29, 1992, in suburban Cobb County, received the most extensive coverage of a local murder by Atlanta media in years. Sara, a white woman, was married to a prominent and ambitious white attorney and Atlanta magistrate (traffic court judge) whose television ads made him recognizable to many area residents. She was shot at close range in the back of the head in front of her two young sons by an African American male. They had just returned from spending Thanksgiving with her parents in Florida.

Sara's husband, Fredric, subsequently was reported to have taken out large life insurance polices on Sara and was implicated in a drug and money laundering ring. Sara had gone to a private investigator with documents indicating, among other things, that he had secret off-shore bank accounts. News reports also claimed that she may have threatened Fredric with her knowledge of his secret papers as a way to gain a divorce and custody. At the time of the interviews, Fredric was considered a prime suspect by police. Since then, Fredric has been charged with murder and has been found guilty on federal racketeering charges.

Testimony from Sara's friends and relatives during the racketeering trial indicated that she was a battered woman who had wanted a divorce but feared Fredric would get custody of the boys because of his connections to influential judges and politicians. The arrested gunman subsequently confessed to the shooting, claiming he was hired by a business associate of Fredric, an African American man who later confessed to having hired the gunman for Fredric. All this was duly reported by Atlanta's news media, which had picked up the story immediately and stayed on it, doggedly pursuing every lead and angle. Media interest in the story has yet to subside and promises to continue when Fredric goes to trial for his wife's murder. Ultimately, if the confessions of the hit man and the man who hired him are true, it matters not whether Fredric pulled the trigger or hired someone else to do the job: Sara's death is gendered within the patriarchal context of an abusive husband exercising final control over his wife.

Given the relatively large number of murders and acts of violence to cover in Atlanta, one might well ask why some crimes of violence are covered and others not. In other words, how do reporters apply standards of newsworthiness as they sift through the many murders, rapes, and other crimes that vie for their attention? What made the murder of a white woman, Sara Tokars, so compelling to reporters, whereas the murders of other women—many of whom are African American, poor, or both—go unreported or underreported?

News organizations whose journalists were interviewed included the *Atlanta Journal/Constitution* (hereafter, *AJC*), which consists of the morning *Constitution*, the afternoon *Journal*, and the Sunday *Journal-Constitution*; two of the three major network television affiliates[4]; two Atlanta radio stations; and the *Marietta Daily Journal*, which, as Cobb County's daily newspaper, covered the murder of Sara Tokars as a local story.[5] Most reporters requested that their names not be used; a few asked that their organizations not be identified. For consistency and so as not to single out those who did not mind being identified, none of the journalists is mentioned by name.

Criteria for selecting journalists were that they had covered crime and either had reported or were familiar with their news organization's coverage of the Tokars case. The journalists were also chosen to represent a cross section of Atlanta's news media. Of the five women and four men interviewed, all were white. The use of an exclusively white pool of reporters was the result of both the lack of minority reporters who covered the Tokars murder and the intent of this study to examine the predominant perspective among journalists regarding news coverage of crimes against women. As a number of researchers have pointed out, the predominant voice within the news is white (Entman, 1990, 1992; Gans, 1980; Shah & Thornton, 1994; van Dijk, 1991).[6]

Reporters were asked about their job responsibilities and routines, factors affecting crime coverage, what details are considered important or unimportant, personal beliefs about objectivity and fairness, whether race and class affected coverage, factors affecting rape coverage, and why the Tokars story generated such heavy coverage. The in-depth interviews, conducted during February 1993, used a 25-item questionnaire as an outline. Frequently, reporters were asked to elaborate on their answers, and often, follow-up questions were asked.[7]

The Interviews

"My job," explained one reporter, "is not to give you my opinion. . . . My job is to give you the facts." Although most reporters would agree with that statement, it belies the reality that some facts become news, whereas other facts do not—that the facts themselves are neither value-free nor neutral, as the reporter's statement would imply.

Just what makes an occurrence news is vague even to journalists, who are unable to articulate why a particular story was chosen over another for coverage. "I can't put my finger on it, although I know it when I see it," explained a reporter. "It's an instinct." Another reporter claimed that reporters "can, after a while, smell what's good (to cover) and what's not." For example, he added, "If you hear a story and you say to yourself, 'Oh, my God,' or 'Gee whiz,' it's a pretty good indicator."

Sorting Through Crimes

The journalists varied in the amount of freedom they had to choose stories. Some said they usually were assigned stories after the news agenda was set at an editorial meeting; others said they mostly decided what to cover on their own, although editors occasionally would hand them a story. General assignment reporters were most often in the former category, and beat reporters were in the latter. Regardless of how reporters came to cover their stories, however, they shared common understandings about newsworthiness and what facts are important to a story.

Although journalists may not be able to define news, they seemed able to agree that certain stories should be covered and certain facts included as opposed to others. This agreement underscores the consensual nature of both the news process and the definition of newsworthiness. For example, one television reporter pointed out that although he and a reporter for another station may cover a murder differently, the story will essentially be the same: "He may start with relatives running up to the house crying, and I may start with investigators bringing the body out. When the story's all said and done, it's going to be essentially the same facts presented in a different way."

Reporters also refer to commonly held news values to explain what constitutes the news. Chief among those values are audience interest, impact—that is, the potential to affect many lives—and timeliness. As the editor noted, the two major factors in deciding what to cover are "how many people are going to be affected by something" and "how many people are going to be interested in something." However, both of those factors need not be present for a story to be considered newsworthy; interest alone may be enough.

Timeliness was also cited by reporters as a factor in determining what is news. But although a story may be timely, that alone won't guarantee coverage. In addition, the amount of interest that news directors think a story will generate—an important factor in ratings—and "visuals" to illustrate the story are of utmost importance in television.

Reporters believe that people are particularly interested in crime in their own neighborhoods and are more likely to talk about the "shooting down the street," as the editor said, than the president's economic plan. Although they claim that violence is of interest to the public, journalists also acknowledge that not all violent crime can be covered simply because of a lack of space and time. Some stories are obviously newsworthy, such as a plane crash, a reporter explained, whereas others are considered newsworthy if they are "very unusual" or "quirky," "something that people will be talking about," "stuff that may show a trend," and "stuff that strikes a chord with people." Stickups, burglaries, and "drug-heads" shooting each other occur so frequently in Atlanta that they hardly warrant coverage, reporters said.

"For radio news," a radio reporter explained, "something unusual or bizarre certainly is going to get a lot more coverage than what we would consider our average, run-of-the-mill type crimes. The oddity would determine how much coverage it would get." The notion of news as oddity or unusual reflects what Roshco (1975) has called the news value of the unexpected, in which "the unexpected is inherently obtrusive" and therefore receives high visibility within the news (p. 16).

Within reporting, a hierarchy of crime exists, with murder considered the most serious crime and, under most circumstances, generating more coverage than other crimes. "If somebody's shot and they don't die, then it's not a story," explained a reporter. "That sounds cold, but that's just the way it works." But not all murders are covered. Domestic violence, even when it results in murder, is considered so common that it does not generally warrant coverage, reporters explained. "If someone gets shot on a street corner and it turns out to be a domestic argument, the chances of that making the air are slim," said a television reporter. Reporters emphasized that only "sensational" or unusual murders are covered because murders occur so frequently in Atlanta.

No matter how odd the crime, however, most stories "grow cold fairly quickly," a reporter said. "It's unusual that you're still writing about a crime a week later." Most reporters admitted that their news organizations could do a better job of following up on crimes. "It gets to be such a huge volume of stuff that only the extremely big cases get the continual follow-ups," a reporter explained. Thus, only the crimes that are unusual or sensational get both initial coverage as well as follow-up.

Competition

Atlanta is considered by reporters to be a very competitive news market, with television station ratings generally within a point of each other. News managers watch other stations' news shows to find out how they did on the same stories and whether they left out any details. "They play the comparison game," acknowledged a TV reporter.

Both *AJC* and radio reporters admitted that they compete with television. Radio reporters said they were more likely to watch television than to listen to another radio station for comparison. Whereas the *AJC*, like radio, considers television its biggest competitor, the *Marietta Daily Journal* is competing with the *AJC*. "If the *Journal-Constitution* does something that I don't have . . . I'd be all over it the next morning," the Marietta reporter said.

The Tokars story was considered by reporters to be "a very competitive story," with every news organization "trying real hard to break out in the front," according to a reporter. "On the Tokars thing, there's been so many angles and twists and turns, everybody's always trying to get an exclusive out of that," he said. "And there's a lot of different back alleys to go up so everyone's always trying to see what they can come up with first."

The newspaper editor credited television with keeping the Tokars story alive and increasing newspaper coverage of it. "We drive television most of the time," she said. "In the case of breaking news, such as that [Tokars] case, in the case of crime news, TV sometimes trumps us." In this way, competition between media outlets—which was not confined to same-medium organizations—fueled the Tokars story, with each new report prompting reporters from other news organizations to attempt to outdo or scoop their competitors.

Police

Reporters frequently mentioned that stories usually have two sides, both of which need to be covered. However, some sides or opinions clearly carry more weight and have more legitimacy than others. In crime reporting, police are the primary and most legitimate source of information. Generally, crime stories are the result of tips from the police or assignments from editors or news directors who might have heard about a crime from people at the scene or from a police scanner.

To do their jobs, crime reporters must develop working relationships with police officers who eventually come to trust them and will provide them with information or access to information. One reporter noted that she tended to talk to the same police officers for stories: "the cops that I know that trust me and will talk to me."

Newsworkers consider police legitimate, unbiased news sources, as opposed to other sources who might be viewed as having a vested interest in a particular outcome. For example, a representative of a rape crisis center might be seen as biased because she advocates for the victims of rape. Quoting her would require the reporter to get an opposing quote to balance the story. As a reporter explained, "We try to stay away from special-interest groups unless we can get more than one group to tell their side of the story." The police, on the other hand, are seen as neutral, so balancing quotations from an opposing perspective is not considered necessary.

Reporters not only depend on the police for story tips and information but they also cooperate with the police in restricting information that might help a suspect or otherwise jeopardize an investigation. "If the police told us not to mention the victim's name," said a reporter, "I wouldn't mention the victim's name—or the suspect's name if they're looking for the suspect. And anything that would affect the case, I wouldn't put in." Such information is provided "off the record" by police. For example, reporters knew within 24 hours of Sara Tokars's killing that the murder weapon was a 410 shotgun. They agreed not to reveal that particular piece of information to the public. When Curtis Rower was subsequently arrested, he told police he had used a 410 shotgun, which helped corroborate his confession.

Despite reporters' needs for information from the police, the relationship is often adversarial. The editor explained:

> It's kind of an odd relationship because the police want to give you stuff sometimes to help them, so that they can put it out there and, you know, they get tips. And then there are certain things they don't want you to know. There's a lot of tension there. It's a push-pull relationship, basically, because they need you sometimes and you need them all the time.

The result is that crime news provided by police officers with whom reporters have established a working relationship tends to reflect the views, assumptions, and opinions of the police.

Rape

Individual rapes are rarely covered by the *AJC* or television, although the Marietta reporter said that she will provide a "brief" for most rapes. For a rape to receive more than that at the Marietta paper, or to be covered at all by the Atlanta news media, the rape would have to have been particularly brutal or unusual, part of a pattern, or it would have to involve a victim who was either very old or very young—or have another criminal aspect to it, such as armed robbery or kidnapping. "There are so many rapes that it would be impossible for time reasons to do them all," explained a television reporter. He added that the circumstances in which the rape occurred determine whether it gets covered. Those circumstances, said a radio reporter, might be "if the person is beaten up badly, gang raped, if it's something like she's been stalked or if it happened in a public place," such as a school, or a place "that you take for granted," such as a parking deck.

The notion of some rapes being more newsworthy than others is, like crime reporting in general, rooted in the idea that only the unusual is worth covering. The emphasis on the uncommon renders most rapes not simply unnewsworthy but unimportant. For the most part, only serial rape is considered newsworthy. Reporters justify coverage of serial rape as a kind of public service to alert women to the dangers of certain areas. "One of the main reasons for doing a story like that is reader service—that women in that area need to know," noted a reporter. However, rapes don't have to be concentrated in a particular location to be reported, according to another reporter, as long as a clear pattern exists: "If he's breaking into second-story apartments with sliding glass doors, then you do a story saying, somewhere, somebody in Atlanta is breaking into second-story apartments with sliding glass doors, and everybody in the city who lives in one needs to be aware of it."

Age may also be a factor in whether a rape is covered. "Old and fragile ladies make the victim even more pathetic"—and, therefore, more newsworthy—a reporter explained. Or as another reporter stated in recalling a story about "a guy who raped old women" in south Atlanta, "Because it was old women in a limited area and it was people we feel sorry for, it gets coverage." The rape of young children is also considered more newsworthy than the rape of women who are young adults or middle-aged.

Rape, then, is newsworthy only if it involves a serial rapist, the rape of someone very old or very young, or what reporters consider unusual circumstances.

Victims

Most of the reporters said that covering crime had made them more sensitive to the plight of the victim and that the crimes that affected them the most involved the abuse or murder of children. Several reporters claimed that they had become more sympathetic to victims as a result of having covered crime over the years, particularly when the crime involved child abuse, sexual abuse, and domestic violence.

Not all reporters sympathized with the victims, however. For example, one reporter said that she takes the "outsider's" point of view" when covering stories rather than taking sides. If she were covering a story about a battered woman, she explained, she would take an "outsider's" perspective that asked "why these patterns start, why these particular behaviors occurred." This supposed outsider's view, however, is not value-free, for often it is based on the police perspective and assumes that the cause of the violence resides within the interactive behavior of the woman and man—a position that implicates the woman in her own abuse. Another reporter emphasized that, with the exception of children, there are few "real" victims:

> Often, people are somewhere that they shouldn't be, doing something that they shouldn't be doing. Some are legitimate victims—they are very few, though. They are either killed in domestic cases, doing drugs, or something like that. This one woman was shot at three times by her husband but didn't leave him. He finally killed her. I just can't sympathize with that.

This reporter, like many of the others interviewed, did not believe that battered women were deserving of sympathy, perhaps because these journalists do not understand how the cycle of violence affects women and the reasons that women remain in abusive relationships—the most obvious reasons being a woman's lack of financial support and the very real fear of being killed or having her children injured if she left. Despite this unwillingness to sympathize with battered women, most journalists said they sympathized with children who are the victims of violence.

Race and Class

Race and class are often conflated by Atlanta reporters as well as by residents. Although Atlanta has a sizable black middle and professional class, it also has a considerably larger population of poor African Americans.[8] These socioeconomic demographics, combined with racial ideology, lead reporters and others to speak of race and class as one—to assume, in other words, that black is synonymous with poor.

Most newsworkers said their organizations had policies concerning mentioning race in a news story. Generally, the race of the victim or suspect is noted only if it is an issue in the story, as in a racially motivated murder or incident or if it will help in the identification of a body. "We've gotta have more than he was a white male, 5-foot-10 inches and wore blue jeans," the editor said. "I mean, that could be . . . everybody who's at Georgia Tech right now. And the same with black males—you know, '21, had an afro.' I mean, that could be anybody. So I leave out descriptions if they are just useless and provide no real direction for the reader."

Editors generally try to be sensitive to "the kind of reaction you can create in the community" by reporting race, the editor added. A radio reporter also noted that the demographics of the city required extra sensitivity on the part of journalists: "We try to be careful about that because we are in a city that has a minority population that is the majority."

Although the race of the victim and assailant are rarely mentioned, newspaper photographs and television visuals are often revealing, as is the location of a crime or the home address of the assailant or victim. Atlanta's neighborhoods are largely segregated, with African Americans to the south and whites to the north, so most residents can fairly accurately guess the race of a suspect or victim by the location of the crime or the home address. For example, the south side of Atlanta is code for black and generally poor, although Southwest Atlanta is home to many middle-class and wealthy African Americans. Atlanta's public housing projects, such as Carver Homes and Bankhead Courts, are considered exclusively black. On the north side of the city, the neighborhood of Buckhead, as well as the northern counties of Gwinnett and Cobb and the suburban community of Dunwoody, are synonymous with rich and white. Regardless of the location of the crime, a reporter pointed out, the general expectation is that the crime has been committed by an African American man: "Everybody knows in 90% of the cases it is a black male."

Most—but not all—of the reporters interviewed denied that race affected coverage. One reporter readily admitted that the crime stories most likely to get covered "are anything where middle-class or a white person is injured or killed or victimized. . . . If you attack poor, black people, the media doesn't care." She noted that the Sara Tokars case is a perfect example of the news media's preference for white, middle-class victims. Another reporter pointed out that the killing of an African American mother in the inner city the night before Sara Tokars was murdered got little coverage. And a third reporter contrasted the Tokars murder with the slaying of two African American children:

> We had a double murder here shortly after the Tokars slaying . . . where two kids were just slaughtered. Their throats were slit. Their mother was a drug dealer, you know, and we did some stories on that. And that crime was 10 times more heinous—it involved children—than the gunshot slaying of Sarah Tokars. . . . These kids were just mutilated, and yet it didn't get the high-profile press that Sarah Tokars got.

However, even those who acknowledge that a discrepancy exists between the coverage of white and black victims of violence claim that the difference can be attributed to the unusualness of the crime. As a television reporter emphasized, the unusualness of the circumstances or the motivation behind the crime is "vastly more important" than race in determining who and what gets covered.

In addition, although reporters admitted that social class plays a role in coverage, they insisted that this was due to the public's interest in prominent people, as well as the unusualness of crimes among the elite. "I think that all of us have a tendency to play it up if there is high society and big money," explained a radio reporter. "Tokars is the best recent example of that."

Crimes that occur in affluent neighborhoods, such as the east Cobb area where Sara Tokars was murdered, are considered unusual and, therefore, worth covering. "Shootings and knifings and all that type of thing are more common in lower-income strata," explained a reporter, "and I guess you don't expect it in the idyllic suburbs. And so when something like that happens, it's out of place. And things that are out of place, in essence, are news." Another reporter claimed

that reporters and the public were intrigued by th
because of the "fairy tale" aspect of the Tokarses' lif
"This doesn't happen to 'nice' people; we expect i
people. We don't expect it from middle-class." T
"low-class people," she added, is the result of news being written
from a middle-class perspective: "You don't have housing project
people writing the news. If you would, you would probably get more
balanced reporting. But most of them can't read, so you see the
problem here."

This reporter was the only one who acknowledged that coverage
is shaped by the class biases of those who produce the news—that is,
middle-class reporters and editors. Other journalists attributed any
class bias in the news to (a) the public's interest in those who are
prominent and wealthy and (b) the fact that crimes among the elite
are considered rare—and therefore more newsworthy.

The Murder of Sara Tokars

Reporters agreed that the Tokars murder had a high media profile
because of Fredric's prominence as a judge and attorney and the fact
that he was a suspect in the murder. One reporter noted that Fredric's
refusal to talk to the media also made them suspicious. And the fact
that Sara was killed in front of her two children made the murder
particularly heinous to reporters. As one reporter stated, the Tokars
murder had a variety of elements that alone warranted extensive
coverage, beginning with the emotional impact of two small children
"seeing mommy get blown away":

> It's in affluent east Cobb, which doesn't have very many murders.
> Probably Cobb police up there haven't worked another murder within
> two miles of there in the last 10 years. The rarity of the crime in that
> area makes it high coverage. And the fact Fredric Tokars is on TV
> looking for business—his social status and notoriety in the commu-
> nity—that would get him coverage by itself. Throw in the nature of the
> crime, the violence with a shotgun to the back of the head—that would
> get coverage anywhere. Add all those things up and you get monumen-
> tal coverage.

A number of reporters explained that the narrative guaranteed the
story exceptional coverage. It provided reporters with the material

with which to tell a good yarn—a "who dunnit," in the words of one reporter—and to continue to tell that story as more information came to light. "It's a story of what seemed to be the all-American family, but something apparently was drastically wrong," said a reporter. There was also, the editor pointed out, the "race factor," which, added to the other elements of the story, heightened public interest:

> You had two black defendants who somehow are connected to a very well-educated white man—her husband. Anything that involves race in our part of the world, I think in the entire United States, creates quite an atmosphere of great interest. I think when you add race and you add money and you add murder and you add children watching their mother get killed, which is what happened in this case, there's going to be a great deal of interest in it.

Discussion

Unusualness was the predominant rationale and guiding principle that reporters cited to explain how they determine which crimes to cover.[9] Crime must be quirky, out of the ordinary, rare, and uncommon to be reported. Because cases of domestic violence and rape are all too common, they can be dismissed by reporters unless they have an unusual twist.

Reporters' notions of newsworthiness as guided by the concept of unusualness reflect both the complexity and interlocking nature of oppression. Patriarchy does not operate independent of racial or class interests; these forms of oppression work together to support, maintain, and reproduce the dominant ideology (Bartky, 1990; hooks, 1992; Meyers, 1994), which is reflected within journalists' collective understandings and beliefs concerning newsworthiness and the nature of news. The rape of elderly women is newsworthy not because they have been raped but because they are "pathetic" and somebody "we feel sorry for." Women who are not elderly but are battered, raped, or even murdered appear to be journalistically unimportant unless they are white and middle-class—or if they can serve as a warning to other women.

Quite simply, news coverage of violent crimes reveals society's biases and prejudices. It tells us who is valued and who is not; whose life has meaning and whose life is insignificant; who has power and who does not. Reliance on the imperative of unusualness not only obscures gender, class, and race bias, it also fosters the use of stereotypic assumptions concerning women, minorities, the poor, and the elderly while underscoring their subordinate positions within a social hierarchy that privileges whites, males, youth, and wealth.

It is worth emphasizing that newsworkers' understandings are not independent judgments but, rather, consensual, derived from their common socialization within the newsroom and the fact that most reporters and editors at mainstream news outlets share the dominant values and ideals of the larger society. Thus, gender, race, and class bias in the news is not necessarily the result of individual sexism, racism, or classism on the part of reporters—although that may contribute to the problem. Rather, the personal prejudices of reporters have less to do with the content of crime news than does the reliance on unusualness as a guiding principle of newsworthiness. The problem, then, is systemic, related more to journalists' common understandings of newsworthiness and news values than conscious intentions and prejudices.

By claiming unusualness as a guiding principle in the determination of coverage, reporters are able to deny that they themselves, and the news organizations they work for, are biased in their coverage. Reporters' inability to define news as other than an instinct, as something that would elicit a "gee whiz," allows them to make collectively subjective decisions based on consensual notions of what is newsworthy. That consensus, although appearing to be based on common sense and what is "natural" (as in, it is natural that the public should be interested in "high society and big money"), reflects the dominant ideology in its underlying assumptions and values. The vagueness of the definition of newsworthiness also contributes to an environment in which, because there are no hard-and-fast rules, reporters can defend choices that, although perhaps not *intentionally* biased by gender, race, and class, become biased in fact.

Reporters cited the number of people affected, the number likely to be interested, and the timeliness of an event as news values that guide them in determining which events become news. However, the emphasis on unusualness contradicts these news values, suggesting that reportorial reliance on unusualness may supersede the news values of effect and interest in the coverage of crime. For if rape and murder in poor, black neighborhoods in and around Atlanta are frequent occurrences, then clearly they affect large numbers of people and would, presumably, be of interest to those who have previously been victimized or are at risk of being affected by crime.

In addition, a number of reporters emphasized that because murders involving drugs are rampant in African American neighborhoods, those killings are undeserving of coverage. The assumption that most murders of African Americans are drug-related reflects the widespread viewpoint among whites that African American neighborhoods are drug infested and African Americans themselves are more prone to use illegal drugs and engage in criminal activities than whites. But it is not drugs that make a crime unnewsworthy—it is who is involved. And if those involved are white and have money, then the crime is likely to be covered.

Although only the last of 25 questions on the questionnaire asked about the Tokars case, newsworkers brought up the Tokars case throughout the interviews to illustrate their points. This, no doubt, reflects the fact that the Tokars murder was the hottest news story going at the time of the interviews and that most of the reporters interviewed had firsthand experience covering it. But it also reflects that, to the newsworkers, the Tokars case illustrated perfectly their rationale of unusualness as a guiding principle in the determination of news and newsworthiness.

What gets covered is also a function of what police think should be covered. Reporters' reliance on police as the primary, legitimate source of information concerning crime lends them a credibility and neutrality that denies that their official perspective may be marked by prejudice, bigotry, and misogyny. Frequently, the police are regarded by workers at rape crisis centers and domestic violence shelters as insensitive to the concerns and needs of raped and battered women. And minority communities have long decried police racism of the sort underscored by the beating of Rodney King by Los Angeles police. That reporters present police views as unbiased is indicative of their influence in determining what crimes and viewpoints are presented to the public. Tuchman (1972) has emphasized that the reportorial mandate to present both sides as a neutral outsider allows reporters to claim objectivity and protect themselves from charges of bias. This study indicates that journalists' conceptions of the unusualness of the crime, coupled with the vagueness of the definition of news, do much the same in protecting them from accusations of bigotry and prejudice where gender, race, and class are concerned.[10] As long as unusualness remains a guiding principle in the reporting of crime news, the news will continue to reflect the biases—and interests—of a patriarchal society.

Notes

1. This is not to suggest that any news is without bias and that there is an objective truth or reality waiting to be uncovered by reporters. Any reality is socially constructed, not the result of objective facts (Berger & Luckmann, 1966), and attempts to examine the news for bias in contrast to objectivity are inherently flawed (Hackett, 1984).

2. The inclusion of a lone editor with eight reporters was not expected to affect the outcome of this study because editors and reporters share a common understanding of news values and goals, as well as newsworthiness (Berkowitz, 1992; Gans, 1980; Sigal, 1973; Tuchman, 1978; Turow, 1994). The editor was included because she had extensive experience covering crime, first as a reporter and, at the time of the interview, as an *Atlanta Journal-Constitution (AJC)* editor whose work included the assigning and editing of crime stories.

3. Although only one question—the last—directly mentioned Tokars, reporters repeatedly drew from her murder to illustrate their points.

4. A reporter for the third affiliate insisted that the station's reporters were prohibited by management from being interviewed.

5. The *Marietta Daily Journal*, with a Sunday circulation of 28,796, is a smaller, more community-based newspaper than the *AJC*, whose Sunday circulation is 700,739 and which covers a broader metropolitan area (circulation figures in Gale, 1993).

6. That voice also is male (Gans, 1980; Rakow & Kranich, 1991; Tuchman et al., 1978; Women, Men and Media Project, 1994).

7. The questionnaire began with general questions about the nature of news and the journalist's job (including the definition of news, the importance of objectivity, how she or he decides what to cover and how to choose sources, what determines the "play" given a story, and the effect of competition), then moved to questions more specifically about crime stories (such as what types of crime stories are most likely to get covered, whether social status is a factor in what crime stories get covered, whether there are certain crime stories that don't get covered, whether race is mentioned in a crime story, what crime stories require follow-up, and whether the journalist thought crime coverage was fair to the victim). The interview concluded with questions specifically about the coverage of violent crimes against women (including what makes a rape story worthy of coverage; whether race, location, age, or social status are factors in rape coverage; and why the Tokars story received such extensive coverage).

8. Just over a quarter (27.3%) of Atlanta's 394,017 residents live below the poverty level, according to the 1990 federal census. Of the 102,364 below the poverty level, 88,718 are black and 11,239 are white.

9. This was true whether the journalist was female or male. In fact, there appeared to be no substantive differences in the comments and views of those interviewed that could be related to gender.

10. The comparison cannot, however, be taken at more than face value. Tuchman's (1972) study focused on the practices of journalists in the reporting and writing of news. This study's focus is on how reporters decide which events should be selected for coverage.

CHAPTER

7

Reforming the News

If the news is to stop contributing to the epidemic of violence against women and actually work to eradicate it, journalists must take responsibility for halting the perpetuation of myths and stereotypes that underlie patriarchal ideology and the mythology of anti-woman violence. They must stop signifying women as good or bad girls, depending on the women's adherence to the rules of appropriate, gendered behavior. They must stop excusing men for their violent behavior. And they must stop blaming the victim and looking to *her* actions for the reason she was abused. In short, the news must be made to, in the words of Ann Jones (1994), "clean up its act" (p. 228).

More often than not, the news is guilty of biased and unfair coverage when reporting male violence against women:

> Too often print and broadcast journalists, male and female, especially crime reporters, fall back on sexist cliches and ready-made scenarios instead of investigating and accurately reporting facts. They mask rape

and battering in the language of "love." They quote police and lawyers as authoritative sources but rarely consult battered women's advocates, who might bring a different perspective to bear on the facts of the story. Sometimes they throw fairness and balance to the winds and sympathize with the offender. (Jones, 1994, p. 228)

This chapter points out ways in which the news can, in fact, "clean up its act." It draws on interviews with 20 advocates who serve rape survivors and battered women in Atlanta and outlying areas. Journalists generally view advocates with suspicion and believe they are a biased special-interest group. They thus tend to ignore women's advocates when covering incidences of rape or battering. However, advocates—many of whom have been the victims of male violence themselves—are usually in the best position to place this violence within a context outside the social mythology and stereotypes. In other words, because of their personal and professional experiences, they are more likely to have a broad, and therefore perhaps more analytical, view of the problem.

This chapter is an attempt to give voice to the experts—the advocates—by presenting their views and recommendations for improving news coverage. It first will present suggestions from researchers and writers who have outlined steps that journalists can take to avoid coverage that is damaging to women. The goal of all these suggestions is to dispel harmful myths and stereotypes while increasing public awareness and understanding.

Mining the Literature

Most of the academic and public debate concerning news coverage of violence against women has focused on whether news organizations should disclose the names of rape victims. This debate becomes most vociferous when a specific, usually sensationalized, case is given extensive media attention. Examples include the coverage of the rape trial of William Kennedy Smith, who was charged with the rape of an identified Patricia Bowman, as well as the case of the Central Park Jogger, the unnamed investment banker who was viciously gang raped and beaten.

The question of victim identification is argued from both ethical and emotional quarters. Some, such as former *Des Moines Register* editor Geneva Overholser, contend that identifying the victim is necessary to destigmatize rape. When Overholser published an editorial in 1990 asking rape victims to come forward with their stories, Nancy Ziegenmeyer volunteered to be the subject of a series about her rape and the subsequent consequences for her and her family. The series won a Pulitzer for the *Register*. Ziegenmeyer has since called the media exposure dehumanizing and has lobbied for laws that would ban the publication of rape victims' identities (Cooper & Whitehouse, 1994).

Helen Benedict (1992) notes three other arguments used by the media to justify their use of victims' names: that they should not be in the business of keeping secrets, that naming victims lends them credibility, and that naming the accused but not the accuser violates the suspect's right to be considered innocent until proven guilty (pp. 252-253). Benedict concludes, however, that these arguments are naive and ignore the sexual humiliation that victims experience. The public exposure of rape victims, she claims, is nothing short of punitive.

Whereas Benedict and other feminists argue against publication of the victims' names, Ann Jones (1994) also suggests that newspapers identify men who are under restraining orders, "calling particular attention to men convicted of violating restraining orders" (p. 228). Jones also urges print and broadcast journalists to educate themselves about male violence against women with a reading list of books on the subject.[1]

Benedict (1992) provides a fairly comprehensive list of both individual and systemic reforms that journalists must undertake to provide coverage that is accurate and fair. Her inventory of reforms includes the following:

- Using vocabulary that avoids words or the suggestion that the woman deserved or enjoyed the assault
- Obtaining balance so that if the victim's sex life is mentioned, the suspect's is also mentioned
- Providing a context with information that allows people to protect themselves
- Being considerate of the families and the victims
- Following up on what happened to the victim and perpetrator

- Developing policies and trainings for reporters and editors so that they learn to recognize myths and stereotypes, as well as their own race, class, and gender biases
- Leaving descriptions of the victims and their behaviors out of the story
- Diversifying the newsroom

She also suggests that journalists emphasize accuracy rather than speed, stop harassing families, and stop blaming sources for biases in reporting and public demand for sensationalism in their stories. In addition, Benedict underscores the need for journalists to consider feminism a legitimate voice and perspective on the issue:

> At the moment, the mainstream press is so unwilling to consult feminist sources that it has effectively crippled its chance of covering sex crime properly, for it is in the fields of feminist sociology, medicine and anthropology that an understanding of these crimes lies. (p. 265)

Carolyn Byerly (1994) also recommends that reporters seek input from sexual-assault experts at rape crisis centers to "supplement the reporter's own knowledge of rape and to provide credible analysis and attribution" (p. 62). She argues that sexual assault stories should provide a context—provided by statistics, research, and other information—to present the "big picture" (p. 62).

Byerly's list of materials appropriate to teach college journalism courses has value for seasoned reporters and editors as well. The list includes (a) state laws on rape and other forms of sexual assault; (b) national, local, and campus statistics on incidence and prevalence of sexual assault crimes; (c) a list of rape and sexual assault terminology; (d) a list of local services for victims, survivors, and families; (e) information on the need for victim confidentiality in news reports; (f) a short handout on rape trauma syndrome; (g) a short history of the antirape movement; (h) a list of campus policies related to sexual offenses in college communities; and (i) a current bibliography on sexual assault (pp. 65-67).

In addition, Byerly suggests story ideas and tips appropriate for student journalists, which also would be useful for professional journalists. These include publishing stories about

> reporting and prosecution rates, local victim or offender treatment programs, local services for families and survivors, and new statewide

rape-related policies and laws. Stories about acquaintance rape should always include background about this being the most common form of sexual assault (particularly on campuses) and why. Story lines and details to avoid in news stories include the victim's dress and lifestyle and the sexual history of the assailant and victim, unless they are central to the legal case. (p. 67)

In his survey of rape survivors, Kevin Stoner (1992) concluded that they deemed stories emphasizing details about the assault or the survivor—such as occupation, age, home address, and physical appearance—inappropriate and an invasion of privacy. On the other hand, survivors supported the inclusion of many details regarding the attacker: race, physical description, how he gained access, whether a weapon was used and what kind it was, and what sort of physical violence was involved.

Stoner, however, did not include the victims of battering in his survey. Indeed, all of the suggestions noted above refer to the coverage of rape and other sex crimes; battering, which has been accorded significantly less attention by news scholars, has been left out. Also missing from the literature are the voices of advocates, except insofar as the researcher also is or has been an advocate.

The Advocates

The remainder of this chapter will present the results of in-depth interviews with 20 female advocates for victims of sexist violence. Half were advocates for rape victims; the other half were advocates for battered women. In many instances, the advocates, all of whom were women, also had been victims themselves. The advocates were either staff, volunteers,[2] or former staff or volunteers for battered women's shelters, rape crisis programs, or other services or organizations whose goal is to help women who are the victims of male violence. The geographic distribution included rural, suburban, and urban advocates in Atlanta and north Georgia, although the metropolitan Atlanta area was more heavily represented.

Racial representation was not a consideration in the choice of advocates. Given the frequently very busy schedules they had, the interviews were conducted with whoever was most available or amenable at a particular agency or organization. Of the 20 advocates interviewed, 4 were African American and the remainder were white. All were promised anonymity.

The advocates were asked their views about news coverage of rape or battering, as well as for examples of coverage they found particularly good or bad. They also were asked for suggestions concerning how coverage could be improved and whether they believed race and class played a role in coverage. The questions were intentionally broad and open-ended both to prevent responses from being circumscribed by the interviewer's opinions or biases and to elicit the widest range of suggestions and comments possible. For example, instead of asking advocates whether training programs for journalists would improve the news, the advocates were asked first if they thought the news could be improved and then, if the answer was affirmative,[3] what that might take.

For the most part, the advocates agreed that, in the words of one, "journalists are just failing us miserably." The primary problem, they claim, is that the media perpetuate myths and stereotypes that ultimately blame the victim. As a rape victim advocate stated,

> I think it (news coverage) perpetuates a lot of stereotypes that are out there—that the woman asked for it, that the woman could have prevented it, that the only rapes that occur are stranger rapes, because they're usually the only ones that are reported. It perpetuates all that in the minds of the public. And you know, that's the big fight that we still fight—which is to try to make society understand what rape is really about. That it's violence, that it's not sex, that it's power and control, that women don't deserve it, no matter what. And as long as the news media is not helping us with that, they're hurting us.

Similar myths, of course, are presented about battered women and women who are the victims of other types of male violence. What's needed, the advocates insist, are reporters and editors who have educated themselves about anti-woman violence and understand that they have a responsibility to educate the public. In essence, explained one advocate, what's required is

> a new breed of reporters who are more concerned with the feelings and recovery of the survivor and less concerned with the shock [value] of presenting all the violence and the facts so that people go, "Wow" or "I can't believe that happened."

Advocates' Suggestions for Improvement

Following are the advocates' more specific suggestions for ways that journalists can improve coverage and, in so doing, contribute to the elimination of male violence against women. Each suggestion represents the concerns of at least two advocates, although it is possible most or all of those interviewed would support the opinions presented had they been asked to comment on specific recommendations rather than come up with their own.

Stop blaming the victim. The most common complaint about news coverage is that it blames the victim. Reporters and editors often look at the woman's actions as the reason for her being attacked and ask what she did to provoke the violence and what she could have done differently to have avoided it. The advocates stated that journalists must become aware of how the framing of their stories fosters stereotypes that make the victim appear to have "asked for it." For example, they should not include irrelevant details—such as what she wore, whether she was dating, what she did, and the like—as rationalizations for the crime.

A frequently used stereotype that blames women, an advocate stated, is that the victims are "sluts." For example, women recently murdered in Atlanta by what appeared to be a serial killer were identified at the very beginning of the stories as prostitutes, another advocate explained. This not only gave other women a false sense of security—"He's only raping prostitutes, so I'm safe"—but it also encouraged people to believe that the women's actions might have been responsible for what happened to them. The fact that the women were prostitutes, the advocate said, could have been downplayed or placed later in the story, so that their actions wouldn't appear to be the cause of their deaths. Responsible journalists, another advocate stated, should

> give the information about the crime, give the information about the perpetrator and what he's been charged with. Don't emphasize so much about the victims and what she was doing and how she got in that situation, because that's not important.

Identify battering for what it is. Often, stories will discuss the murder of a woman by her partner as just another murder, without placing it in the context of battering, advocates claimed. This denies the pain and abuse that battered women endure, and it makes the cause of death appear inexplicable or the result of a man's suddenly having "snapped." Reporters also frequently describe the murder of women by boyfriends or husbands as "crimes of passion" or the result of obsessive love. These murders, advocates said, should be identified for what they are—final attempts to control, manipulate, torture, abuse, and own women.

A number of advocates also suggested that journalists avoid the terms *domestic disturbance, domestic dispute,* or *domestic violence.* Such terms hide the social context in which this violence occurs, masking the fact that women are far more often the victims and that men are the perpetrators. By obscuring who is at fault, the news represents the crime as independent of other such crimes and divorced from larger issues concerning power and control within a patriarchal society.

Cover everyday, run-of-the-mill violence against women, not just celebrity or sensational violence. A number of advocates noted that the news emphasizes celebrity cases while ignoring the fact that women are murdered, battered, and raped by men every day. They pointed out that news reports of Nicole Brown Simpson's murder and O. J. Simpson's trial presented the case as an aberration, something that just doesn't happen very often. The rape trials of William Kennedy Smith and Mike Tyson, they added, similarly led people to conclude that rape is an anomaly.

Advocates for rape survivors also point out that when the news does report noncelebrity rape cases, it focuses on stranger rapes rather than the far more common acquaintance, spousal, or incest rapes. This, they state, not only posits stranger rape as the norm but also as the only real, authentic rape, thereby isolating women who are raped by a family member, acquaintance, or someone else they know. Survivors of nonstranger rape thus may be more likely to believe that they are somehow at fault because their experience has not been legitimated as rape by the media. Responsible coverage, the advocates suggest, should accurately portray the number of women who are raped and the conditions under which those rapes occurred.

Let the victim tell her own story. Although, obviously, this is not possible when the woman has been murdered, victims of battering or rape can present the reality of violence against women in a way that journalists cannot. A number of advocates noted that the media's best coverage of violence against women comes from talk shows or editorials in which the women are able to tell in their own words what happened to them and how that has affected and continues to affect their lives and families. Advocates suggested that more could be done along these lines with news stories that provide space for victims of anti-woman violence to speak out.

Put a face on the victim and her family—but only if she (or her family if she is no longer alive) agrees. Advocates were split on whether to avoid most details about the victim as a way to protect her anonymity and privacy or whether to "paint a face" on the victim, as one advocate stated, so that she and her pain become more real and accessible to news audiences. But even those who favored "humanizing" the news by making the victim appear "real" agreed that the first priority should be to protect the victim and honor her wishes.

Details that could be used, if the victim was amenable, include the impact of the violence on the victim and on her children, parents, and others, as well as her progress in healing. The key, said one advocate, is to let the public know that the victim was a human being who was cared for and who cared for others.

Stop including details that will identify, humiliate, embarrass, or otherwise discomfit the victim. This requires that reporters be sensitive to what the victim may or may not want reported. Advocates gave numerous examples of stories in which details should have been left out because they were unnecessary and served primarily to embarrass or "revictimize" the woman. For example, one advocate complained that her local newspaper printed details such as that the perpetrator "stole her underwear or that she had several bruises on her bottom—just things it's not necessary for the public to know that are embarrassing for the survivor."

In addition, although newspapers may avoid publishing the victim's name, they sometimes provide enough other details, such as her age and the apartment complex where she lived, that "you already know who it is," an advocate noted. Another advocate stated that some details, such as that a woman was using illegal drugs at the time she was assaulted, not only blame her for the abuse but also can cause problems for the victim at home if her family was not aware that she was taking drugs. A third advocate felt that details such as the victim's asking her assailant to use a condom are also unnecessary and could confuse the public, which may view her request as indicative of consensual sex.

Educate themselves about violence against women. Advocates emphasized the need to sensitize journalists to anti-woman violence. Reporters, they said, need to educate themselves about the myths concerning sexist violence so that they don't perpetuate them. The advocates suggested that reporters read books about violence against women, conduct interviews and have discussions with advocates and the victims of battering and rape, and participate in training programs for volunteers at rape crisis centers or shelters for battered women. News organizations, some suggested, could help by establishing training programs similar to family violence programs for police.

Educate the public about violence against women. Rather than personalizing coverage so that each incident of violence against a woman appears to be isolated, such violence should be presented within the larger social context of patriarchy, a number of advocates said. For example, one explained that battering should be portrayed as a social rather than an individual problem between two people who cannot communicate; rape should be portrayed as an attempt to humiliate and control women rather than as a man's uncontrollable desire for sex.

In battering cases, one advocate suggested, reporters could provide more details and information concerning earlier instances of violence that led up to the act that finally made the news. Presenting the violence within its ongoing context, she added, rather than presenting the act of violence that was reported as an aberration or the result of the perpetrator's having suddenly and inexplicably become homicidal, would help explain the cycle of battering, its escalating nature, and why women stay in abusive relationships.

Similarly, advocates suggested that journalists could explain how the law enforcement, judicial, and social service systems fail women. This would help the public understand how women are let down by the police and courts and why women often feel forced to remain with abusive men. An advocate explained:

A lot of these women are going to the system, but they're not getting any help. They are being turned away. They are being told, "I don't know where you can go" or "I'm sorry, you don't have any grounds for this; you don't have any grounds for that." And the next thing you know, they're dead.

Advocates also wanted stories to include information about how to prevent or halt violence against women, as well as a list of services and resources for women who have been the victims of violence.[4] In addition, advocates recommended that journalists use them or other experts on rape and battering as sources in every story about violence against women so that reporters and the public receive better information about the dynamics and context of this violence.

Stop portraying rape victims as liars. Rape victim advocates noted that rape coverage is unlike the coverage of any other crime because it often questions the veracity of the victim and presents her as potentially lying. "They leave that impression in the reader's mind, and they don't do that with other alleged crimes," an advocate stated.

She added that rapes that fit the "stranger rape" stereotype and in which the victim has suffered significant physical damage are considered more credible than acquaintance or spousal rape. "Society as a whole still thinks rape is OK unless it happens to you by a stranger and you were doing everything completely right," another advocate explained.

Take violence against women as seriously as other types of violence. Violence against women should be represented as wrong and should not be excused, minimized, or presented as the mutual responsibility of both the man and the woman, advocates said. It should be given the same coverage accorded violence among males or strangers rather than being ignored because it is considered too "common" or private.

One advocate noted that news coverage of property crimes committed in Atlanta during Freaknik, an annual gathering of black college students from around the United States, was far more extensive than the numerous Freaknik-related rapes and sexual assaults. She noted that the number of rape cases increased dramatically during Freaknik, with 80% of those reported at a downtown rape crisis center being related to the event. The numerous incidents of sexual harassment during Freaknik—"women whose clothes were stripped off . . . and malicious behavior toward women"—were also downplayed in the news, which focused instead on a few isolated incidents of looting and vandalism.

Be sensitive to issues of race and class. Advocates disagreed about some of the effects of race and class on coverage, but most concurred that poor women and women of color are at a disadvantage when it comes to news reports of violence against them. Some maintained that crimes by black men are more likely to be reported; others said this was the case only if the victim was white. A few advocates claimed that the news media are not interested in black-on-black violence against women, particularly when the woman is poor, and that violent crimes against white women are more likely to be covered. "If the jogger in Central Park had been black," commented an advocate, "she wouldn't have gotten the coverage that she got when she was attacked."

Others said that white women, particularly those with financial resources, are most able to stay out of the news, whereas black women, particularly if they are poor, are most likely to be exploited by the news media. One advocate stated that although white, middle- and upper-class women may not be able to avoid being covered, they are most likely to receive favorable reporting:

> An upper-class white woman is probably going to receive much more coverage, much more balanced coverage, in a newspaper article if she is a victim, as opposed to someone who is poor or who is using drugs or prostituting or doing other things that might be considered marginal or criminal activities.

Another advocate said upper-class white men are often able to keep their names out of the news when they engage in violent crimes against women: "There are probably a lot of wealthy white men in this community that are child molesters or rapists or batterers that we don't ever hear about."

Reporters, advocates agreed, should be sensitive to the issues of race and class so that they do not exploit or treat unfairly poor women and women of color. News organizations can facilitate the process by establishing policies that ensure fairer coverage to all women who are the victims of male violence.

Stop letting men off the hook. The opposite side of blaming the victim for having been abused is that men are absolved of responsibility for their actions. By focusing on the woman's actions and situation rather than on the man's choice to be violent, advocates said, the man frequently escapes blame and responsibility for his violence. One advocate noted that the myth that men cannot help themselves gives them "permission to not be in control of themselves." Another advocate stated,

> I think many of the articles are written in a way that's very embarrassing and derogatory towards the survivor and almost written so that you feel sorry for this poor guy—"Oh, how could she accuse him of doing this? How could she say that he would do this?"

Getting It Right

Advocates found the vast majority of news coverage of violence against women to be in need of major repair. As a group, they were hard-pressed to think of examples of good reporting. However, a few acknowledged that a rare journalist had succeeded in fairly and accurately reporting about anti-woman violence. Those stories, they said, can make a difference in the public's perception of violence against women and, as a result, in the public's response. For example, one advocate recalled that news coverage of the murder of a woman in Gainesville, Georgia, spurred the community into at least talking about what actions it could take to make women safer:

> In Gainesville several years ago, a woman was killed. She had all the legal protection. Her husband came to her office, literally threw the secretary out, pulled the phone out of the wall, and shot her. The local media covered that story; it talked very honestly about [how] the legal protection she had was just a piece of paper, that the courts, the law enforcement had done everything they could to protect her; that she had done everything that she could to protect herself. They then talked about what else needs to happen. And the community at that point started looking at the need for counseling for batterers: "Is that going to change [anything]? Is that going to make any difference in providing safety?" And it really was because of the media's coverage. That really helped.

News stories such as this one—that seek to educate the public rather than blame the victim and that refrain from the invocation of stereotypes and the disclosure of unnecessary and damaging details—can have a positive impact on a community. Right now, advocates and researchers agree, such stories constitute a small minority of the coverage of anti-woman violence. These stories go against the grain, challenging the myths and assumptions that predominate in most news coverage of violence against women.

The suggestions provided by the advocates indicate actions that journalists and news organizations can take to improve their coverage. Much needs to be done, but the task is not impossible. Stories such as the one about the murdered woman in Gainesville provide evidence of this. What is needed, quite simply, is a whole lot better reporting by a whole lot more journalists. Listening to victims and advocates is the first step.

Notes

1. The books on this list are *Battered Wives*, by Del Martin (1976); *Women and Male Violence*, by Susan Schechter (1982); *Rape in Marriage*, by Diana E. H. Russell (1982); *Violence Against Wives*, by R. Emerson Dobash and Russell P. Dobash (1979); *When Battered Women Kill*, by Angela Browne (1987); and *Virgin or Vamp: How the Press Covers Sex Crimes*, by Helen Benedict (1992).

2. Interviewed volunteers included members of the boards of directors of organizations that work with raped or battered women, as well as volunteers providing more direct services to the victims of male violence.

3. All respondents answered that question affirmatively.

4. One advocate suggested that information about battering and where to go for help should be presented on children's television programs so that they can urge their mothers to get help.

Conclusion

Journalists may claim that they are merely reflecting society and therefore cannot be held accountable for its ills. However, the news is not neutral, in either its representation or its effects. It shapes our understanding of the world around us in subtle and not so subtle ways, and we act on those understandings. When the news portrays female victims of male violence as responsible for their own abuse, when it asks what a woman has done to provoke or cause the violence, when it excuses the perpetrator because he was "obsessed" or "in love" or otherwise "could not help himself," when it portrays him as a monster or a psychopath while ignoring the systemic nature of violence against women, the news is part of the problem.

The representation of violence against women as separate, discrete incidents reinforces the idea that this violence is a matter of isolated pathology or deviance, related only to the particular circumstances of those involved and unconnected to the larger structure of

117

patriarchal domination and control. In maintaining this mirage of individual pathology, the news denies both the social roots of violence against women and that individual incidents of abuse are part of a larger social problem. This denial works to absolve society of any obligation to end it.

In addition, by drawing on the "virgin-whore" or "good girl-bad girl" dichotomy, the news separates women into categories based not on the guilt or innocence of their assailants but on women's perceived culpability in contributing to the violence. Children and elderly women, because they are presumed to be weak and vulnerable, are generally considered innocent victims. Women who are the victims of serial rapists or murderers or who have been brutalized or murdered in a particularly gruesome fashion, also tend to be cast within the news as innocent. However, even these women can be deemed guilty of causing their own demise if they have transgressed the boundaries of acceptable female behavior.

When victims are not considered frail or helpless, if they do not appear to be too old or too young to defend themselves, they are likely to be blamed for their own victimization. When women fight back against male violence, their actions are judged on the basis of social expectations of "appropriate" female behavior. When those who fight back violate the rules governing this behavior—when they drink or use drugs, marry men much younger than themselves, go out alone at night, or otherwise engage in acts that society considers dangerous, questionable, or unacceptable for women—they may be viewed as using excessive or unnecessary force in defending themselves. On the other hand, women who have not flouted the rules may be portrayed as justified in fighting back.

In reality, the rules of socially appropriate behavior for women do not protect them from male violence. Even women who appear to take every precaution—locking doors and windows, not venturing out unescorted at night, avoiding "dangerous" neighborhoods and activities—may be raped, battered, and murdered. The rules merely serve to reinforce traditional gender roles and keep women in a subordinate position. They also work to cast groups of women against each other, which is, of course, in the interests of patriarchy. Thus, women who are not the victims of male violence (at least, not this time) can take false comfort in the belief that *they* are safe or can remain safe if they behave themselves and act appropriately at all times. The solution to sexist violence lies not in rigid adherence to a belief that protection and safety can be guaranteed by the rules but in exposing the rules for what they are and dismantling the ideology of anti-woman violence.

Race and Class

Representations of women as victims of violence are also tied to discourses of race and class as well as of age and any number of other signifiers of domination and inequality. Within news coverage of violence against women, male and white supremacist ideologies converge. White women are most likely to be covered by the news when they are the victims of male violence, especially if they are middle- or upper-class. Black victims of sexist violence, particularly if they have few financial resources, are simply not seen as newsworthy.

The racial disparity in the coverage of female victims of male violence was evident in the pool of stories available for analysis in this book. During the period when research data were collected, the murder of Sara Tokars was the biggest story, in terms of ongoing coverage and the amount of news generated. Similarly, Katrine Bursheim and the woman who attacked a man believed to be the Buckhead rapist generated the most news coverage involving women who fought back. Not surprisingly, Tokars, Bursheim, and the Buckhead woman are all white.[1]

This is certainly not to suggest that stories about violence against African American women do not make their way into the news. However, those stories are generally not given the high profile of stories about violence against middle- and upper-class white women. The relative invisibility of African American women in this way is a sign of both their comparatively low social ranking and the news media's bias in terms of race and class.

What coverage there is about male violence directed at African American women is shaded by both racist and male supremacist ideologies. The result is that the news draws on and reinforces stereotypes about African Americans and violence, drug abuse, and prostitution. For example, in the story about the African American baby sexually abused and murdered by her father, the representation of the father drew on and reinforced racist stereotypes linking black masculinity with violence and sexual excess. In addition, news reports about the two young African American girls whose throats were slashed shortly after the Tokars murder suggested that the execution-style killings were carried out because their mother was a drug dealer. The news also stated that the mother often was not home and left the girls to fend for themselves. This reinforces the stereotype of African Americans as criminals and drug addicts as well as inadequate mothers.

Details surrounding the act of violence, such as the woman's use of drugs or alcohol or her engagement in prostitution or other illegal or dangerous activities, serve to blame the victim (or her mother) while deflecting responsibility from the real criminal. When such details are mentioned within the context of other, nonsexist crimes—the murder of a man by another man, for instance—they have different meanings because their representation does not carry the weight of the same cultural stereotypes. A man, for example, would probably not be considered foolhardy and irresponsible for being attacked while walking alone at night.

The damage done by bad news coverage is twofold. At the macrolevel, it contributes to the social problem of violence against women by perpetuating myths and stereotypes that are misogynistic and hostile to women. On the microlevel, it directly hurts the victim—and those who care about her. The pervasiveness of the message of blame leaves many women feeling responsible and guilty for their victimization, while at the same time it denies them the full support of family and friends who wonder if she helped cause the violence. In addition, the notion that the woman must have done something to provoke the assault is the reason that police, juries, judges, and attorneys are often more likely to believe the assailant than the victim.

Given the sorry state of news coverage of violence against women, one might well wonder if it would be better for the news media to just not cover crimes such as rape and battering, as was largely the case 20 years ago. This, however, is no solution. Leaving violence against women out of the news simply ignores the problem and creates the impression that it does not exist or, if it does, is not serious enough to warrant coverage. It also isolates women who are the victims of male violence while contributing to the public's misperceptions about who are the victims and perpetrators as well as where and when this violence is most likely to occur.

The perception that the woman is to blame is a result of the *context* within which information is reported rather than simply the inclusion of irrelevant or harmful details about the victim or the act of violence itself. The context, as well as the absence of other information that would explain the violence as the result of patriarchy and male supremacy, sets the stage for blaming the victim. The solution, therefore, may be not so much to eliminate the facts surrounding sexist violence if they concern the woman's actions—although that certainly may be the best alternative in some cases—but to reframe that information so that it does not appear to be the cause leading up to the abuse. What is needed, then, is for journalists to place violence against women within its social context of misogyny and a man's attempt to control, humiliate, dominate, and hurt a woman.

In addition, the public disclosure of details that do *not* blame the victim—such as the extent of injuries, the specific nature of the sexual violence committed, the fact that the assailant took her underpants—also can be damaging to the victim, causing her and her family embarrassment and shame. As a number of advocates for raped and battered women emphasized, those details do more harm than good in news stories and should be omitted.

By citing unusualness as a guiding principle in the determination of coverage, journalists are able to deflect charges of racism and classism, as well as sexism, in their coverage. Because rape, battering, and other acts of violence aimed at women by men are all too frequent, reporters say, these crimes are simply not newsworthy unless they have an "unusual" twist. This is particularly true of violence in African American communities, which is viewed by reporters as so common as to be virtually unreportable.

The convergence of racial and male supremacist ideologies reflected within the news is also shaped by journalists' reliance on the police as the primary, legitimate source of crime news. Police views and opinions, which traditionally have been hostile toward female victims of male violence as well as toward African Americans,[2] predominate. The perspectives of advocates who work on a daily basis with the victims of this violence, on the other hand, are viewed with suspicion and generally ignored.

Because of their work and the fact that many of these advocates have been the victims of male violence themselves, they are in a unique position to provide journalists with an analysis of and a context for understanding sexist violence. They also could provide basic information about anti-woman violence—such as the cycles of violence and the dangers of couple counseling for battered women[3]—that could literally make a life-or-death difference in the decisions women make. Journalists, however, consider advocates to be biased sources whose use would require an opposing perspective for "balance."

Balance and Objectivity

The ideal of journalistic balance or objectivity, however, is a red herring. In practice, it means that reporters should get both sides of a story, balancing the views of a Republican with a Democrat, the opinions of a right-to-lifer with a pro-choice advocate. Gay Tuchman (1972) has noted that the invocation of objectivity serves to protect reporters and editors from charges of bias in reporting. However, it does far more than that. It circumscribes the two sides chosen as the only appropriate ones to be considered, which leaves out any number of alternative possibilities. Perhaps even more insidiously, it proclaims that all acts and statements can be balanced, that there is a legitimate other way to look at things.

Contrary to journalistic lore, there are not always two equally weighted sides to everything. Journalists, who have been socialized to unquestioningly seek objectivity through balance, must recognize that, in most cases, anti-woman violence cannot be balanced. Attempting to do so denies the seriousness of violence against women and raises questions about the woman's behavior in provoking the attack.

Thus, when Dennis Walters pointed a gun to Wanda Walters's head and pulled the trigger in an attempt to terrorize and dominate her, his actions were characterized as merely testing her "toughness." Under the rules of objectivity—that is, getting both sides—the reporter was then obligated to indicate ways in which Wanda similarly tested Dennis's toughness. The result was that Dennis's pointing a gun at Wanda's head and pulling the trigger became equivalent to Wanda's staying out late at night or her choice of clothing and jewelry. Their actions clearly were not equal, either in behavior, intent, or effect. To present them as such obscures the dissimilarity and Dennis's true intent, which could only be to further his control of Wanda by making her fear for her life.

Looking for Why

Reporters and editors also err when looking for the "why" of a story about violence against women. As all reporters know from their earliest days in journalism school, the "five Ws and H"—who, what, when, where, why, and how—provide the cornerstone of good reporting. However, when journalists attempt to establish the why of a story about sexist violence in terms of the woman's actions or the abuser's psyche, they most often miss the mark. The real why behind sexist violence is that men believe that they have the right to control women. This belief is steeped in patriarchal notions of appropriate gender roles and reflects male supremacist ideology.

Of course, some men do murder, rape, or otherwise assault women because they are psychopaths. But most often, their pathology is cultural, reflective of a society that devalues and hates women, that views women as an appropriate repository for male rage and blame. The fact that many men reject sexist violence and that some even work to eliminate it[4] is evidence that sexist violence is an individual choice made—or not made—by men. Until journalists refuse to excuse men for their violence, until they point to misogyny and patriarchy as the why of anti-woman violence, the news will continue to blame women for their victimization while absolving men of responsibility.

Is Change Possible?

It is important to remember that the overwhelming majority of reporters and editors draw on the mythology of anti-woman violence not because they are engaged in a grand conspiracy or consciously seek to maintain male supremacist ideology (although there is no question that some journalists do use their positions to further their own political and personal agendas) but because they, like everyone else, exist within patriarchy, within a culture that views women as subordinate to men. To view the world otherwise is to question the assumptions and ideas on which society rests.

The prevailing myths and ideas about women, men, and violence, as well as those concerning race, age, and sexual orientation, are the glue that keeps patriarchy—and society as we know it—in place. Recognizing the existence of patriarchal myths and stereotypes within the news is the first step toward changing the representation of violence against women. The next step is for journalists to refuse to buy into and perpetuate the mythology.

What is the likelihood that reporters and editors will change their ways? Can they put aside or modify some of the most basic journalistic precepts—such as the mandate that news must be unusual and appear objective and balanced—to more accurately and fairly cover violence against women? Will they be willing to omit details that provide more titillation than insight and that primarily serve to blame the victim? Are they able to frame violence against women within the context of patriarchy and misogyny by providing room for the opinions and views of advocates for women?

The answer to these questions, I believe, is that it is entirely possible for journalists to clean up their act. Indeed, a few of the 20 advocates for battered and raped women from throughout northern Georgia—admittedly a minority of those interviewed—pointed to a reporter or a story that stood out as exemplary. The reporters in that category, they said, were sensitive to the needs and concerns of abused women, avoided further victimizing them through the use of unnecessary details, and relied on advocates for background and context within their stories.

This is cause for hope. What is needed is for reporters and editors to become educated about violence against women and to become more sensitive to both the victims and the effects of coverage on the victim and the community. In addition, as Pauline Bart and Patricia O'Brien (1985) emphasize, the news media should dispel myths about self-defense by providing information that can actually help women avoid being victimized:

> The fact that it is possible to avoid rape when attacked should be widely disseminated, particularly in the mass media. News magazines and television should report in detail instances of rape avoidance so women can learn what works. (p. 118)

The process of education can—and should—take several forms. Journalists can take the initiative by reading about violence against women, attending talks and lectures on the topic, interviewing advocates for women who have been assaulted, and even enrolling as volunteers in training sessions for rape crisis centers and battered women's shelters. In addition, the management of news organizations can establish training programs for employees that draw on the expertise of advocates, victims, and even researchers. News organizations can also establish, and enforce, policies and guidelines for the coverage of anti-woman violence.

Without these changes, women who are the victims of male violence will continue to be revictimized by the news media. And the news will continue to play its role in the perpetuation of both the mythology of anti-woman violence and the violence that stems from it.

Notes

1. The Buckhead woman was not identified by race. However, news footage of the neighborhood and its residents—all of whom were white—created the impression that the woman who defended herself was white as well.

2. The problem of racial bias among Atlanta police officers is in all probability considerably less severe than in cities that do not have an African American police chief and an integrated force, as does Atlanta.

3. Groups such as the Atlanta-based Men Stopping Violence, Inc., which works with men who batter, maintain that couples counseling does not work when there is abuse and inequality of power within a relationship—which is characteristic of battering. They point out that the woman is not free to discuss what is really going on when her batterer is in the counselor's room with her. In addition, women are often beaten when they leave the counseling session because of what they did or did not say.

4. The goal of groups such as Men Stopping Violence in Atlanta and Emerge in Boston is for men to take responsibility for ending anti-woman violence.

Appendix

Editor's Note: Reprinted with permission from The Atlanta Journal and The Atlanta Constitution. Pomerantz, G. (1990).

'90 Georgia falls to LSU 18-13; Tech rallies past N.C. State

▸Florida 50
Okla. St. 7

▸Virginia 20
Clemson 7

▸S. Miss. 27
Alabama 24

▸BYU 28
Miami 21

▸Oilers will find out:
Are Falcons for real?

The Atlanta Journal
THE ATLANTA CONSTITUTION

Copyright © 1990 The Atlanta Journal and The Atlanta Constitution

SUNDAY, SEPTEMBER 9, 1990

$1.25

*****

'I've never loved anybody like that girl . . . Never like this'

Walters family affair: A fatal attraction

By Gary Pomerantz
Staff writer

Dennis Walters was a man of obsessions. Nothing owned his spirit like the Civil War and his fourth wife, Wanda.

The first was the vehicle for his rise, the latter for his fall. He had fought City Hall in a reverse-discrimination suit and won, claiming the job of his dreams in 1985, as Cyclorama director. In his final act, he used a blue-steel Colt revolver to fight his personal obsession and destroyed himself and Wanda Cooper Walters, whom he had adopted as his daughter at age 14.

As his daughter, Wanda Cooper once colored her blond hair red to please him, and often snuggled close to him while his third wife was in the room.

His two-year marriage to Wanda was a civil war in itself.

A month ago today, when she was moving out — wearing his mother's diamond-studded necklace — Mr. Walters carried out his murder-suicide plan in the driveway of their Decatur home. He was 46. She was 23.

Some familiar with the relationship were less than stunned. As an acquaintance said, "When I heard about it, I thought, 'So that's where all of this was leading.'"

Said Jim Walters, his younger brother: "This story is 50 times more involved than anyone will ever know."

The Walterses had been separated for nearly two months. Their divorce was pending. Mrs. Walters had a boyfriend, and her husband brooded over it.

Both were known to be hotheaded and prone to jealousy.

Please see WALTERS, A8 ▸

Walters: In the end, his love consumed them both

► Continued from A1

The mother of Wanda Cosper, Louvale Westbrooks — shown here with a grandchild — caught Dennis Walters and her 14-year-old daughter having sex.

Nick Arroyo/Staff

Mrs. Walters told friends and family members that her husband had played Russian roulette with her, pointing a gun at her head and clicking the trigger. Mr. Walters told her brother, Jesse, that he had only a dud bullet in the gun and was merely testing his wife's toughness.

At other angry moments, Mr. Walters reminded her of her roots and said he would build a "little white-trash room" where she could go when she wanted to act like her family. The Cospers were infuriated by the superior bearing of Mr. Walters, who hailed from a solidly middle-class family.

But Wanda Cosper Walters could test her husband's toughness in other ways. In the months before the separation, Mrs. Walters — wearing the fancy dresses her husband had purchased for their social events — often left alone for the evening for an unannounced destination, Jim Walters recalled. She would return home after midnight. During the separation, she occasionally stopped at her husband's home at 6 a.m. to shower before leaving for her job as a bank teller. (It was a job she later lost because of tardiness, she told her sister.) Dennis Walters fumed through it all.

Recently, Jim Walters had overheard Mrs. Walters playfully tell her estranged husband, "Maybe after we're divorced we can start dating again."

Dennis Walters was "an intense historian, the son of a career accountant for a refining company. He twice had been passed over for the Cyclorama job. In both instances a black was hired. He charged discrimination and a court agreed, awarding him $227,000 and the directorship of the museum that depicts the Battle of Atlanta. "The job was definitely an obsession with him," said Harriet Sanford, director of the Atlanta Bureau of Cultural Affairs and Mr. Walters's boss. His focus and ambition induced then-Mayor Andrew Young, during depositions in the suit, to call him "a nut."

Mr. Walters once said he had yearned to direct Cyclorama since he was 10. Soon after claiming the position, which in 1985 paid a $23,100 salary, he astounded observers by handpainting the tarnished brass cannons that stand in front of the 100-year-old painting of the battle. He painted them gold, contending they were new cannons at the time and would not yet

have tarnished.

Wanda Cosper was the 12th of 14 children from a broken family in Atlanta that long has remained in the grips of poverty.

The retelling of their relationship brings chills: In 1981, Mr. Walters and his third wife adopted Wanda Cosper at age 14. Weeks later, Miss Cosper showed birth control pills to her friend in the ninth grade, Tammi Wolfe, and said, "Dennis took me to a doctor to get me these." Jim Walters observed the relationship and said it didn't take a smart man to see what was happening.

Her mother, Louvale Westbrooks, said she once caught her 14-year-old daughter having sex with Dennis Walters. She chased him, swinging a mallet — and this was before she consented to the adoption. "Wanda said if we didn't sign the papers we'd never see her or hear from her again," Mrs. Westbrooks said. "We were giving Wanda what she wanted."

Dennis Walters divorced his third wife in 1985 and later signed over his adoptive rights to Miss Cosper's stepfather — who believed he was signing insurance papers — in order to marry her. At the time of their May 1988 marriage, he was 44, she was 21.

As man and wife: Dennis and Wanda Walters married in May 1988 and died last month.

The couple attended her five-year high school reunion last summer.

"This is my husband, Dennis," Mrs. Walters proudly told her Roosevelt High Class of '84 classmates. From the background, someone chided, "I thought he was your father!" She bowed her head in embarrassment, and he stared at his shoes.

After they separated, he paid $85 to join a dating service on his brother's advice, telling him he sought "a mature woman in her 30s with two kids, around 10

years old." He had not yet had a date when he died.

*   *   *

The Cosper family has known hardship for decades. J.W. Cosper, the father of Wanda and 11 of her siblings, worked as a carpenter when he could.

He divorced Louvale Cosper, she recalled, in 1969. Martha Cosper, now 26, remembers later standing in a soup line with her father, whom the family considered a loner.

"At times, our family has had almost nothing," Martha Cosper said. "I remember my mother asking at churches for food, money and clothes."

When Mr. Cosper died of natural causes at age 65 last year, his children were surprised to find he had saved their photos and letters from years ago in a foot locker.

For seven years Mrs. Westbrooks and her second husband, Elmer, have lived in a house in southeast Atlanta. They have no telephone. For the first six months of this year, the home had no running water, according to city Water Bureau records. Mrs. Westbrooks said the state took away her eldest five children in 1957, and that she doesn't know where several of her 14 children are today.

"We ain't got money, but we've got common sense and each other," said Jesse Walter Cosper, who at 39 is the oldest of Mrs. Westbrooks's 14 children.

He said he rediscovered his mother in 1980 after a long search.

*   *   *

Wanda Cosper Walters's first attempt to assert her independence fell prey to Dennis Walters's obsession. When she moved away in 1985, Mr. Walters, then her father, followed her closely. She became a bank teller and roomed with former classmate Tammi Wolfe. At night, the women would see Mr. Walters's car parked across the street from their apartment.

Once, Ms. Wolfe recalls, an enraged Mr. Walters broke down their door and began beating his adopted daughter because she had been dating another man. "Wanda told me to call the police, but Dennis pulled two phones out of our wall," Ms. Wolfe said. Despite the outburst, Wanda Cosper left with Mr. Walters that night. Ms. Wolfe moved out the next day.

Jim Walters said: "D told me recently, 'I've never loved anybody like that girl. I'd thought I'd been in love before, but never like this.'"

Dennis Walters — whose boss said he was obsessed with his job at the Cyclorama — was "very sad" after criticism by city officials in 1985, the year he won a reverse-discrimination suit to get the museum directorship.

File

Dennis Walters grew his sideburns long in 1971 for a meeting with David "Carbine" Williams, the long-whiskered inventor of carbine weapons.

Jim Walters believes his brother ultimately was broken by the notion of having lost his wife to another man. When Dennis Walters told his brother he planned to kill his wife, Jim Walters didn't believe him. "Surely, you won't let Wanda win the last hand," said Jim Walters, 43.

Dennis Walters responded, "Yeah, but that would be a helluva price for her to pay."

When Wanda Cosper Walters arrived the night of Aug. 9 to pick up her belongings from Mr. Walters's home, she brought several relatives with her. According to police reports and interviews with witnesses, she and her husband began to argue. Her boyfriend's name was mentioned. Dennis Walters had been drinking. Something snapped. He angrily flung several bags filled with her things. He shattered two of her favorite candy jars. She aimed her tan dress shoes at his favorite lamp, but missed, hitting him. "Let's go, Wanda!" Martha Cosper pleaded. "It's not worth it!"

Mr. Walters retrieved the Colt revolver from under his mattress. On the adjacent nightstand was a picture of his 11-year-old daughter, born of his third marriage.

Mrs. Walters walked toward her boyfriend's car. Her sister and an 11-year-old niece, Elizabeth, were on the other side of the car. Her boyfriend, who had urged her not to go to the house, waited at her apartment.

Mr. Walters had five bullets in the gun. He shot four into his wife and saved the last one for the right side of his head, just behind his ear. She died instantly. He died 24 hours later. The way her lifeless body sprawled on the driveway — an arm across her chest, her legs crossed — reminded Martha Cosper of the way her little sister slept.

Mr. Walters apparently had planned the tragedy. Six days earlier, he had written his first will and had it witnessed by two Cyclorama employees. He kept it in his office and placed a copy at home, in his sock drawer. His brother believes he was not of sound mind at the time.

The final paragraph read: "The pain and destruction that Wanda and I caused each other and others must stop now before anyone else is hurt. I love Wanda with all of my heart and cannot bear to be without her. May God have mercy on both of our souls."

In his will, Dennis Walters requested a double funeral.

Mrs. Westbrooks refused. "Could you blame me?" she said.

Before Mrs. Walters's casket was closed, her tearful boyfriend, Imran Merchant, placed inside a rose, a balloon that read "I Love You" and a picture of himself. Mrs. Walters had called for a family meeting to tell her of her plans to marry Mr. Merchant, a 23-year-old Indian national.

Mr. Merchant, a metro Atlanta courier, has a photo of Mrs. Walters on the dashboard of his car. He said he visits her grave almost every night. "I stand there, and I curse her for not coming back," he said, wiping away tears, "and I curse God."

The 95-degree heat was oppressive the day Mrs. Walters was buried next to her father. More than a dozen cars pulled off the country road into the small cemetery across from New Hope Baptist Church. Those in attendance stared mostly at the sky or the grass.

Dennis Walters was laid to rest near his parents. His funeral was not announced in the newspaper. Only a select few attended.

She was buried in Fayetteville. He was buried in Decatur.

The distance between their graves is about 30 miles.

References

Althusser, L. (1971). Ideology and ideological state apparatuses. In *Lenin and philosophy and other essays* (pp. 127-186). New York: Monthly Review Press.

Avis, J. M. (1991, May). *Current trends in feminist thought and therapy: Perspectives on sexual abuse and violence within the family.* Paper presented at the International Colloquium of Women in Family Therapy, Copenhagen, Denmark.

Bannister, S. A. (1991). The criminalization of women fighting back against male abuse: Imprisoned battered women as political prisoners. *Humanity and Society, 15*(4), 400-416.

Barak, G. (1994). Media, society and criminology. In G. Barak (Ed.), *Media, process, and the social construction of crime: Studies in newsmaking criminology* (pp. 3-45). New York: Garland.

Bart, P. B., & Moran, E. G. (1993). *Violence against women: The bloody footprints.* Newbury Park, CA: Sage.

Bart, P. B., & O'Brien, P. H. (1985). *Stopping rape: Successful survival strategies.* New York: Pergamon.

Bartky, S. L. (1990). *Femininity and domination.* New York: Routledge.

Benedict, H. (1992). *Virgin or vamp: How the press covers sex crimes.* New York: Oxford University Press.

Berger, P. L., & Luckmann, T. (1966). *The social construction of reality.* New York: Doubleday.

Berkowitz, D. (1992). Non-routine news and newswork: Exploring a what-a-story. *Journal of Communication, 42*(1), 82-94.

Bograd, M. (1988). Feminist perspectives on wife abuse. In K. Yllö & M. Bograd (Eds.), *Feminist perspectives on wife abuse* (pp. 11-26). Newbury Park, CA: Sage.

Browne, A. (1987). *When battered women kill.* New York: Free Press.

Brownmiller, S. (1975). *Against our will: Men, women and rape.* New York: Simon & Schuster.

Brummett, B. (1991). *Rhetorical dimensions of popular culture.* Tuscaloosa: University of Alabama Press.

Brunsdon, C., & Morley, D. (1978). *Everyday television: "Nationwide."* London: BFI.

Bumiller, K. (1990). Fallen angels: The representation of violence against women in legal culture. *International Journal of the Sociology of Law, 18,* 125-142.

Byerly, C. (1994). An agenda for teaching news coverage of rape. *Journalism Educator, 49*(1), 59-69.

Byerly, C. (in press). New, feminism and the dialectics of gender relations. In M. Meyers (Ed.), *Mediated women: Representations in popular culture.* Cresskill, NJ: Hampton Press.

Caputi, J. (1993). The sexual politics of murder. In P. Bart & E. Moran (Eds.), *Violence against women: The bloody footprints* (pp. 5-25). Newbury Park, CA: Sage.

Cate, R. M., Henton, J. M., Koval, J., Christopher, F. S., & Lloyd, S. (1982). Premarital abuse: A social psychological perspective. *Journal of Family Issues, 3,* 79-90.

Chancer, L. S. (1987, September). New Bedford, Massachusetts, March 6, 1983-March 22, 1984: The "before" and "after" of a group rape. *Gender and Society, 1*(3), 239-260.

Chibnall, S. (1977). *Law-and-order news.* London: Tavistock.

Cohen, S., & Young, J. (1973). *The manufacture of news: Deviance, social problems and the mass media.* London: Constable.

Collins, P. H. (1993). The sexual politics of black womanhood. In P. Bart & E. Moran (Eds.), *Violence against women: The bloody footprints* (pp. 85-104). Newbury Park, CA: Sage.

Cooper, C., & Whitehouse, V. (1994, August). *To name or not to name: Yes, no . . . maybe so: Questions to ask when the story is rape.* Paper presented at the annual meeting of the Association for Education in Journalism and Mass Communication, Atlanta, GA.

Davis, A. Y. (1981). *Women, race and class.* New York: Random House.

Davis, A. Y. (1989). *Women, culture, and politics.* New York: Random House.

DeLauretis, T. (1987). The violence of rhetoric: Considerations on representation and gender. In *Technologies of gender* (pp. 31-50). Bloomington: Indiana University Press.

Dobash, R. E., & Dobash, R. (1979). *Violence against wives.* New York: Free Press.

Dworkin, A. (1981). *Pornography: Men possessing women.* New York: Perigee.

Edwards, A. (1987). Male violence in feminist theory: An analysis of changing conceptions of sex/gender violence and male dominance. In J. Hanmer & M. Maynard (Eds.), *Women, violence and social control* (pp. 13-29). Atlantic Highlands, NJ: Humanities Press International.

Edwards, S. M. (1987). "Provoking her own demise": From common assault to homicide. In J. Hanmer & M. Maynard (Eds.), *Women, violence and social control* (pp. 152-168). Atlantic Highlands, NJ: Humanities Press International.

Encyclopedia of Southern Culture. (1989). Chapel Hill: University of North Carolina Press.

Entman, R. M. (1990). Modern racism and the images of blacks in local television news. *Critical Studies in Mass Communication, 7*(4), 332-345.

Entman, R. M. (1992). Blacks in the news: Television, modern racism and cultural change. *Journalism Quarterly, 69*(2), 101-113.

Epstein, E. J. (1974). *News from nowhere.* New York: Vintage.

Ericson, R. V., Baranek, P. M., & Chan, J. B. L. (1987). *Visualizing deviance.* Toronto: University of Toronto Press.

Ewing, C. P. (1987). *Battered women who kill: Psychological self-defense as legal justification.* Lexington, MA: Lexington Books.

Fair, J. E. (1993). The women of South Africa weep: Explorations in gender and race. *Howard Journal of Communication, 4*(4), 283-294.

Federal Bureau of Investigation. (1993). *Uniform crime reports, 1992.* Washington, DC: Author.

Federal Bureau of Investigation. (1994). *Uniform crime reports, 1993.* Washington, DC: Author.

Ferraro, K. (1993). Cops, courts, and woman battering. In P. B. Bart & E. G. Moran (Eds.), *Violence against women: The bloody footprints* (pp. 165-176). Newbury Park, CA: Sage.

Finn, G. (1989-1990). Taking gender into account in the "theatre of terror": Violence, media and the maintenance of male dominance. *Canadian Journal of Women and the Law, 3*(2), 375-394.

Fiske, J. (1994). *Media matters.* Minneapolis: University of Minnesota Press.

Fortune, M. (1990). A response to the massacre of women students at the University of Montreal. *Working Together, 10*(2), 1.

Gale Research, Inc. (1993). *Gale directory of publications and broadcast media.* Detroit: Author.

Gans, H. J. (1980). *Deciding what's news.* New York: Vintage.

Gardner, C. B. (1990). Safe conduct: Women, crime, and self in public places. *Social Problems, 37*(3), 311-328.

Giles-Sims, J. (1983). *Wife battering: A systems theory approach.* New York: Guilford.

Gillespie, C. K. (1989). *Justifiable homicide: Battered women, self-defense and the law.* Columbus: Ohio State University Press.

Gilligan, C. (1982). *In a different voice.* Cambridge, MA: Harvard University Press.

Gilroy, P. (1987). *There ain't no black in the Union Jack: The cultural politics of race and nation.* Chicago: University of Chicago Press.

Gitlin, T. (1980). *The whole world is watching.* Berkeley: University of California Press.

Gordon, M. T., & Riger, S. (1989). *The female fear.* New York: Free Press.

Gramsci, A. (1971). *Selections from the prison notebooks.* London: Lawrence & Wishart.

Gramsci, A. (1983). *The modern prince and other writings.* New York: International Publishers.

Gray, H. (1989). Television, black Americans and the American dream. *Critical Studies in Mass Communication, 6*(4), 376-386.

Hackett, R. A. (1984). Decline of a paradigm? Bias and objectivity in news media studies. *Critical Studies in Mass Communication, 1*(3), 229-259.

Hall, S. (1977). Culture, the media and the "ideological" effect. In J. Curran, M. Gurevitch, & J. Woollacott (Eds.), *Mass communication and society* (pp. 315-348). Beverly Hills, CA: Sage.

Hall, S. (1980). Encoding/decoding. In S. Hall, D. Hobson, A. Lowe, & P. Willis (Eds.), *Culture, media, language* (pp. 128-138). London: Hutchinson.

Hall, S. (1981). The whites of their eyes: Racist ideologies and the media. In G. Bridges & R. Brunt (Eds.), *Silver linings: Some strategies for the eighties* (pp. 28-52). London: Lawrence & Wishart.

Hall, S. (1982). The rediscovery of "ideology": Return of the repressed in media studies. In M. Gurevitch, T. Bennett, J. Curran, & J. Woollacott (Eds.), *Culture, society and the media* (pp. 56-90). London: Methuen.

Hall, S. (1986). Variants of liberalism. In J. Donalds & S. Hall (Eds.), *Politics and ideology* (pp. 34-69). Milton Keynes, UK: Open University Press.

Hall, S., Connell, I., & Curti, L. (1977). The "unity" of current affairs television. *Working Papers in Cultural Studies, 9*, 51-93.

Hall, S., Critcher, C., Jefferson, T., Clarke, J., & Roberts, B. (1978). *Policing the crisis: Mugging, the state and law-and-order*. New York: Holmes & Meier.

Hanmer, J., & Maynard, M. (1987). Introduction: Violence and gender stratification. In J. Hanmer & M. Maynard (Eds.), *Women, violence and social control* (pp. 1-12). Atlantic Highlands, NJ: Humanities Press International.

Harlow, C. W. (1991). *Female victims of violent crime*. Washington, DC: U.S. Department of Justice, Bureau of Justice Statistics.

Hart, B. (1989, Winter). National estimates and facts about domestic violence. *NCADV Voice*, p. 12.

Hartley, J. (1982). *Understanding news*. London: Methuen.

Hartmann, P., & Husband, C. (1974). *Racism and the mass media*. London: Davis-Poynter.

Heath, L., Gordon, M. T., & LeBailly, R. (1981, July). What newspapers tell us (and don't tell us) about rape. *Newspaper Research Journal, 2*, 48-55.

hooks, b. (1992). *Black looks: Race and representation*. Boston: South End.

Jones, A. (1980). *Women who kill*. New York: Holt, Rinehart & Winston.

Jones, A. (1994). *Next time she'll be dead: Battering and how to stop it*. Boston: Beacon.

Koss, M. P. (1993). Rape: Scope, impact, interventions, and public policy responses. *American Psychologist, 48*(10), 1062-1069.

Kozol, W. (1995). Fracturing domesticity: Media, nationalism, and the question of feminist influence. *Signs, 20*(3), 646-667.

Kramarae, C. (1981). *Women and men speaking: Frameworks for analysis*. Rowley, MA: Newbury House.

Lemert, J. B. (1989). *Criticizing the media: Empirical approaches*. Newbury Park, CA: Sage.

Long, K. (1990, August 11). Cyclorama chief tries to end life of battles. *Atlanta Constitution*, pp. D-1, 6.

Loseke, D. R. (1989). "Violence" is "violence" . . . or is it? The social construction of "wife abuse" and public policy. In J. Best (Ed.), *Images of issues: Typifying contemporary social problems* (pp. 191-206). New York: Aldine de Gruyter.

Lubiano, W. (1992). Black ladies, welfare queens and state minstrels: Ideological war by narrative means. In T. Morrison (Ed.), *Race-ing justice, en-gendering power: Essays on Anita Hill, Clarence Thomas, and the construction of social reality* (pp. 323-363). New York: Pantheon.

Mahoney, M. R. (1991, October). Legal images of battered women: Redefining the issue of separation. *Michigan Law Review, 90*(1), 1-94.

Makepeace, J. (1981). Courtship violence among college students. *Family Relations, 30*(1), 97-102.

Malamuth, N., Haber, S., & Feshback, S. (1980). Testing hypotheses regarding rape: Exposure to sexual violence, sex difference, and the "normality" of rapists. *Journal of Research in Personality, 14*, 121-137.

Malette, L., & Chalouh, M. (1991). *The Montreal massacre.* Charlottetown, Prince Edward Island: Gynergy Books.

Martin, D. (1976). *Battered wives.* New York: Pocket Books.

Matthews, N. A. (1993). Surmounting a legacy: The expansion of racial diversity in a local anti-rape movement. In P. B. Bart & E. G. Moran (Eds.), *Violence against women: The bloody footprints* (pp. 177-192). Newbury Park, CA: Sage.

Meyers, M. (1992). Reporters and beats: The making of oppositional news. *Critical Studies in Mass Communication, 9*(1), 75-90.

Meyers, M. (1994). News of battering. *Journal of Communication, 44*(2), 47-63.

Mills, K. (1988). *A place in the news: From the women's pages to the front page.* New York: Dodd, Mead.

Molotch, H. L. (1978). The news of women and the work of men. In G. Tuchman, A. K. Daniels, & J. Benet (Eds.), *Hearth and home: Images of women in the mass media* (pp. 176-185). New York: Oxford University Press.

Molotch, H. L., & Lester, M. (1974). News as purposive behavior: On the strategic use of routine events, accidents and scandals. *American Sociological Review, 39*(1), 101-112.

Morley, D. (1980). *The "nationwide" audience: Structure and decoding.* London: Methuen.

Morley, D. (1985). Cultural transformations: The politics of resistance. In M. Gurevitch & M. Levy (Eds.), *Mass communication review yearbook* (pp. 237-250). Beverly Hills, CA: Sage.

Mouffe, C. (1981). Hegemony and ideology in Gramsci. In T. Bennett, G. Martin, C. Mercer, & J. Woollacott (Eds.), *Culture, ideology and social process* (pp. 219-234). London: Open University Press.

Pagelow, M. D. (1981). *Woman-battering: Victims and their experiences.* Beverly Hills, CA: Sage.

Painter, N. I. (1992). Hill, Thomas, and the use of racial stereotype. In T. Morrison (Ed.), *Race-ing justice, en-gendering power: Essays on Anita Hill, Clarence Thomas, and the construction of social reality* (pp. 200-214). New York: Pantheon.

Pharr, S. (1988). *Homophobia: A weapon of sexism.* Inverness, CA: Chardon.

Pharr, S. (1991). Redefining hate violence. *Transformations, Little Rock, ARK: Women's Project, 6*(2), 1-2, 10.

Pomerantz, G. (1990, September 9). Walters family affair: A fatal attraction. *Atlanta Journal and Constitution,* pp. A-1, A-8.

Rakow, L., & Kranich, K. (1991). Woman as sign in television news. *Journal of Communication, 41*(1), 8-32.

Rape in America: A report to the nation. (1992, April 23). Prepared by the National Victim Center in Arlington, Virginia and the Crime Victims Research and Treatment Center of the Department of Psychiatry and Behavioral Sciences at the Medical University of South Carolina, Charleston.

Rapping, E. (1994). *Media-tions: Forays into the culture and gender wars.* Boston: South End.

Reynolds, L. (1987). *Executive summary of the Second National Workshop on Female Offenders,* Raleigh, NC.

Roshco, B. (1975). *Newsmaking.* Chicago: University of Chicago Press.

Russell, D. E. H. (1982). *Rape in marriage.* New York: Macmillan.

Russell, D. E. H. (1984). *The politics of rape: The victim's perspective.* New York: Stein & Day.

Ryan, W. (1971). *Blaming the victim.* New York: Pantheon.

Saltzman, L. E., Mercy, J. A., Rosenberg, M. L., Elsea, W. R., Napper, G., Sikes, R. K., Waxweiler, R. J., & the Collaborative Working Group for the Study of Family and Intimate Assaults in Atlanta. (1990). Magnitude and patterns of family and intimate assault in Atlanta, Georgia, 1984. *Violence and Victims, 5*(1), 3-17.

Sanders, M., & Rock, M. (1988). *Waiting for prime time.* New York: Harper & Row.

Schechter, S. (1982). *Women and male violence.* Boston: South End.

Schudson, M. (1978). *Discovering the news.* New York: Basic Books.

Schwengels, M., & Lemert, J. B. (1986, Spring). Fair warning: A comparison of police and newspaper reports of rape. *Newspaper Research Journal, 7,* 35-42.

Scully, D., & Marolla, J. (1993). "Riding the bull at Gilly's": Convicted rapists describe the rewards of rape. In P. B. Bart & E. G. Moran (Eds.), *Violence against women: The bloody footprints* (pp. 26-46). Newbury Park, CA: Sage.

Shah, H., & Thornton, M. C. (1994). Racial ideology in U.S. mainstream news magazine coverage of black-latino interaction, 1980-1992. *Critical Studies in Mass Communication, 11*(2), 141-161.

Sheffield, C. J. (1987). Sexual terrorism: The social control of women. In B. Hess & M. Ferree (Eds.), *Analyzing gender: A handbook of social science research* (pp. 171-189). Beverly Hills: Sage.

Sheffield, C. J. (1993). The invisible intruder: Women's experiences of obscene phone calls. In P. Bart & E. Moran (Eds.), *Violence against women: The bloody footprints* (pp. 73-78). Newbury Park, CA: Sage.

Sherizen, S. (1978). Social creation of crime news: All the news fitted to print. In C. Winick (Ed.), *Deviance and the mass media* (pp. 203-224). Beverly Hills: Sage.

Sigal, L. (1973). *Reporters and officials: The organization of politics and newsmaking.* Lexington, MA: D. C. Heath.

Smart, C., & Smart, B. (1978). Accounting for rape: Reality and myth in press reporting. In C. Smart & B. Smart (Eds.), *Women, sexuality and social control* (pp. 89-111). London: Routledge & Kegan Paul.

Soothill, K., & Walby, S. (1991). *Sex crime in the news.* London: Routledge.

Spelman, E. V. (1988). *Inessential woman: Problems of exclusion in feminist thought.* Boston: Beacon.

Stanko, E. A. (1985). *Intimate intrusions: Women's experience of male violence.* London: Routledge & Kegan Paul.

Stark, E., & Flitcraft, A. (1988). Violence among intimates: An epidemiological review. In V. B. Hasselt, R. L. Morrison, A. S. Bellack, & M. Hersen (Eds.), *Handbook of family violence* (pp. 293-317). New York: Plenum.

Stark, E., Flitcraft, A., Zuckerman, D., Grey, A., Robison, J., & Frazier, W. (1981). *Wife abuse in the medical setting: An introduction for health personnel* (Monograph No. 7, Office of Domestic Violence). Washington, DC: Government Printing Office.

Stoltenberg, J. (1989). *Refusing to be a man: Essays on sex and justice.* Portland, OR: Breitenbush.

Stoner, K. (1992). The effect of rape stories on survivors: Listening to other voices. *Feminisms, 5*(1), 3-12.

Stout, K. D. (1991). Women who kill: Offenders or defenders? *Affilia, 6*(4), 8-22.

Totman, J. (1978). *The murderess: A psychological study of criminal homicide.* San Francisco: R & E Research Associates.

Tuchman, G. (1972). Objectivity as strategic ritual: An examination of newsmen's notions of objectivity. *American Journal of Sociology, 77*(4), 660-679.

Tuchman, G. (1978). *Making news: A study in the construction of reality.* New York: Free Press.

Tuchman, G., Daniels, A. K., & Benet, J. (1978). *Hearth and home: Images of women in the mass media.* New York: Oxford University Press.

Turow, J. (1994). Hidden conflicts and journalistic norms: The case of self-disclosure. *Journal of Communication, 44*(2), 29-46.

U.S. Bureau of the Census. (1990). *1990 census of population and housing: Summary population and housing characteristics, Georgia.* Washington, DC: U.S. Department of Commerce.

U.S. Department of Justice. (1991). *Crime in the United States, 1990.* Washington, DC: Author.

U.S. Department of Justice. (1992). *Crime in the United States, 1991.* Washington, DC: Author.

U.S. Department of Justice. (1993). *Crime in the United States, 1992.* Washington, DC: Author.

U.S. Department of Justice. (1994a). *Crime state rankings.* Washington, DC: Author.

U.S. Department of Justice. (1994b). *Violence against women: A national crime victimization survey.* Washington, DC: Author.

U.S. Department of Justice. (1994c). *Violence between intimates.* Washington, DC: Author.

van Dijk, T. A. (1985). Introduction: Levels and dimensions of discourse analysis. In T. A. van Dijk (Ed.), *Handbook of discourse analysis: Vol. 2. Dimensions of discourse* (pp. 1-11). London: Academic Press.

van Dijk, T. A. (1988a). *News analysis: Case studies of international and national news in the press.* Hillsdale, NJ: Lawrence Erlbaum.

van Dijk, T. A. (1988b). *News as discourse.* Hillsdale, NJ: Lawrence Erlbaum.

van Dijk, T. A. (1991). *Racism and the press: Critical studies in racism and migration.* London: Routledge.

van Zoonen, L. (1994). *Feminist media studies.* London: Sage.

Walker, L. E. (1979). *The battered woman.* New York: Perennial Library.

Walker, L. E. (1984). *The battered woman syndrome.* New York: Springer.

Walker, L. E. (1989). *Terrifying love: Why battered women kill and how society responds.* New York: Harper & Row.

Women, Men and Media Project. (1994). *Arriving on the scene: Women's growing presence in the news.* Alexandria, VA: Unabridged Communications.

Women, Men and Media Project. (1995). *Slipping from the scene: News coverage of females drops.* Alexandria, VA: Unabridged Communications.

Zelizer, B. (1992). CNN, the Gulf War, and journalistic practice. *Journal of Communication, 42*(1), 66-81.

Zelizer, B. (1993). Journalists as interpretive communities. *Critical Studies in Mass Communication, 10*(3), 219-237.

Index

About the Author

MARIAN MEYERS, Assistant Professor in the Department of Communication at Georgia State University, is a former reporter and news editor.

She has been involved with battered women's movement since the mid-1970s, when she was among the first group of volunteer trainees at Daybreak, a shelter for battered women and their children in Worcester, Massachusetts, and was a member of the steering committee of the Massachusetts State Coalition of Battered Women's Service Groups. Most recently, she has served on the board of Men Stopping Violence in Atlanta, Georgia.

Besides the examination of news coverage of violence against women, her research interests include the mediated representation of women and other socially marginalized groups within popular culture.